AFRIKANER AND
AFRICAN NATIONALISM

AFRIKANER AND AFRICAN NATIONALISM

South African Parallels and Parameters

EDWIN S. MUNGER

Published for the
Institute of Race Relations

OXFORD UNIVERSITY PRESS
1967

Oxford University Press, Ely House, London W.1

GLASGOW NEW YORK TORONTO MELBOURNE WELLINGTON
CAPE TOWN SALISBURY IBADAN NAIROBI LUSAKA ADDIS ABABA
BOMBAY CALCUTTA MADRAS KARACHI LAHORE DACCA
KUALA LUMPUR HONG KONG TOKYO

*Printed in Great Britain by Richard Clay (The Chaucer Press), Ltd.,
Bungay, Suffolk*

CONTENTS

ACKNOWLEDGEMENTS

The seed for this book was sown by the request of Professor Kalman Silvert of the American Universities Field Staff for a short chapter on South Africa in the A.U.F.S. volume edited by him[1]. Although rewritten, reordered, and much expanded, the author's debt to Dr. Silvert's conceptualization of nationalism is gratefully acknowledged. Parts of that chapter are included through permission of Random House and with appreciation to Editor Jess Stein. The encouragement for a fuller study was provided by Philip Mason of the Institute of Race Relations in London.

In an effort to be as accurate as to facts and as balanced in judgement as possible on a highly controversial subject, drafts of this book have been commented on by a number of people with particular expertise. Quite candidly, nearly all the Afrikaners consulted felt the manuscript was too critical of Afrikaners and greatly over-emphasized the importance of African nationalism. Conversely, liberal critics, both white and African, suggested stronger criticism of Afrikanerdom and a greater emphasis upon the African struggle for equal rights. Obviously, no one but the author should be blamed for the result.

A prominent Afrikaner, a leading African nationalist, and others made valued criticisms, but, because of their political or official roles, asked not to be identified. The author is deeply grateful to them and to the following: Professor Jeffrey Butler, a South African now teaching political science at Wesleyan University; Judge Victor Hiemstra; Professor A. C. Jordan, formerly of the University of Cape Town, and now teaching African Literature at the University of Wisconsin; Otto Krause, editor of *News/Check* magazine in Johannesburg; Professor Leonard Thompson, Professor of African History at U.C.L.A., also formerly of Cape Town University; Professor Edward Tiryakian, Professor of Sociology, at Duke University; Professor F. A. van

[1] *Expectant Peoples: Nationalism and Development*, New York, Random House, 1963.

Jaarsveld of the University of South Africa; Willem van Heerden, Editor in Chief of *Dagbreek Pers*; and Quintin Whyte, Director of the South African Institute of Race Relations in Johannesburg. None have seen the revised manuscript. Their sharp differences in viewpoint are immediately evident to students of South Africa. None should be deemed guilty of association with individuals of opposing political views.

The author is likewise most grateful to his research assistant, Margaret Shepherd, and to Simon Abbott and Claire Pace of the Institute of Race Relations in London for their editing of the manuscript.

Pasadena, California   E.S.M.
February 1967

INTRODUCTION

'South Africa is unique.' This is the one observation common to South Africa's most bitter critics and impassioned defenders. Critics are generally those who view the present state of affairs as one of power concentrated in the hands of a white oligarchy. Defenders emphasize the past (how South Africa got where she is today) or the future (the dire consequences for all South Africans and the western world if the critics have their way).

South Africa's uniqueness has many roots. The Afrikaner is a man of Africa, not a settler. Nowhere else in the world are the majority of citizens denied political participation on the basis of class, religion, race, or ethnic origin. The division of English versus Afrikaner has analogies elsewhere, such as with the Walloons and Flemish in Belgium. Colour stratification of white and black is sometimes analogous with the American South or, more subtly, the North. The juxtaposition of both patterns in South Africa is unique. South Africa is a developed nation by most criteria, with an average increase of gross national product of 6 per cent annually in recent years. Nationalism or political development in the usual sense has not been a prerequisite for economic growth, although it is likely that further economic development must await at least partial solutions to political problems.

For these and other reasons much of the literature of development by such leading analysts as Walter Rostow, James Coleman, Gabriel Almond, Lucian Pye, Edward Shils, Kalman Silvert, and David Apter is applicable only in part to this case.

South Africa also has a novel role in relation to the colonialism that blanketed most of the developing world until after the Second World War. Some of the concepts developed by O. Mannoni, based on Madagascar,[1] and the reflections of Philip Woodruff on British rule on another continent,[2] cast fascinating sidelights on British colonialism of Afrikaners in South Africa as well as on Afrikaner relations with

---

[1] *Prospero and Caliban: The Psychology of Colonization*, New York, Praeger, 1956: London, Pall Mall, 1965.

[2] *The Men Who Ruled India*, 2 vols., London, Cape, 1953–4: New York, St. Martin's Press, 1954.

Africans. The phenomenon of ambivalent feelings towards those they governed by officials in India has a parallel in the fact that some of the staunchest behind the scenes supporters of some avenues of African advance in South Africa are those Afrikaner officials most intimately associated with Africans. But on balance one does not draw useful analogies from general colonial experience of recent decades or centuries of British relations with its 'white' colonies and dominions. The author has noted in both Liberia and Ethiopia certain parallels with the Republic based on a common lack of recent rule by a European colonial power, but they are peripheral to the pattern of nationalisms in South Africa.

General works on African nationalism are unsatisfactory in their treatment of either white or black nationalism within the Republic. Such a distinguished professor as Hans Kohn, whose seminal writings on the growth of nationalism in Europe pioneered this field, is not at his top form when he comes to discussing South Africa. In *African Nationalism in the Twentieth Century*, which Kohn wrote with Wallace Sokolsky,[1] the authors make a number of questionable assertions such as: 'It is a crime in South Africa to advocate political, economic, or social change.' This would be news to the Progressive Party which advocates the immediate admission of Africans with primary school education to the voting rolls, to such a staunch Afrikaner as Anton Rupert, who advocates employment of capital in the Transkei irrespective of the race of the man possessing it, and to the Nederduitsche Gereformeerde Kerk as well as the Anglican and Catholic Churches, all of whom advocate sweeping changes, or at least investigations into the system whereby Africans are 'endorsed out' of urban areas and families sometimes separated.

Understandably, continental approaches to nationalism in Africa rest primarily on the emergence of 'black Africa', with much less attention to northern Africa and a one-sided view of South Africa. This is true of the otherwise excellent *The Political Awakening of Africa*,[2] edited by Rupert Emerson and Martin Kilson, whose sole inclusion on South Africa is the 'Indictment of South Africa' by Nelson Mandela in his famous trial speech.

[1] New York, Van Nostrand, 1965.
[2] New York, Prentice Hall, 1965.

Emerson points out in his thoughtful chapter, 'Nation-Building in Africa',[1] that 'North Africa has shaped peoples which have a sense of national identity, and in South Africa the Afrikaners have produced the most intense and coherent nationalism on the continent'.

Thomas Hodgkin has long been one of the most original students of nationalism in Africa. In *Nationalism in Colonial Africa*,[2] he employed the term 'nationalist' to cover all individuals or groups who asserted the rights of an African society against European overlords. There was a time during the British hegemony when Afrikaner nationalists would have accepted and come within that definition, although Hodgkin restricted his terminology to colonial Africa.

The South African scene itself has been well, if unevenly, lit from many angles. Poetry – poignant, descriptive, or fiercely political – has been the finest and truest outlet of Afrikaans literature until the recent advent of *die sestigers* (novelists of the sixties). 'English' South Africa is best delineated by novelists and short story writers (has any community produced so many outstanding women writers from one million people?).

The classic histories of South Africa include the brilliant drawing together of certain main strands by C. W. de Kiewiet in *A History of South Africa: Social and Economic*,[3] W. M. MacMillan's *Bantu, Boer and Briton*,[4] and the longer work of Eric Walker with its plethora of detail, *A History of South Africa*.[5] Leo Marquard has condensed South African history in *Peoples and Policies of South Africa*,[6] while Leonard Thompson has written a contemporary political history in *Republic of South Africa*.[7] The latter accounts are by deeply knowledgeable historians who are in sharp disagreement with present trends in the land of their birth. Even more critical is sociologist Pierre L. van den Berghe's *South Africa, A Study in Conflict*.[8]

---

[1] Karl W. Deutsch and William J. Foltz, Eds., *Nation-Building*, New York, Atherton Press, 1963: London, Prentice Hall, 1964.

[2] London, Muller, 1956.

[3] London, Oxford University Press, 1941.

[4] London, Faber, 1929.

[5] London, Longmans, 2nd. ed., 1940.

[6] London, Oxford University Press, 2nd. ed., 1960.

[7] Boston, Little, Brown, 1966.

[8] Middletown, Wesleyan Press, 1965.

Among early commentators, James Bryce is less successful than on America. None the less, his *Impressions of South Africa*,[1] relating his travels in 1895 when South Africa was unformed, foresaw that 'Twenty years hence the white population is likely to be composed in about equal proportions of urban and rural elements . . . but both these sections will have one thing in common. Both will belong to an upper stratum of society; both will have beneath them a mass of labouring blacks, and will therefore form an industrial aristocracy resting on Kaffir labour.'

Olive Schreiner, the first of South African women writers to achieve world fame with her *Story of an African Farm*,[2] was even more foresighted in her little known *Thoughts on South Africa*,[3] in which she sympathetically analyses the Boers and their aspirations. But no early observer of South Africa was as prescient as Lord Tweedsmuir, best known to some as a Governor-General of Canada and to others as the author of *The Thirty-Nine Steps* and other mystery thrillers. As John Buchan he was in Lord Milner's 'kindergarten'. In his *The African Colony: Studies in the Reconstruction*[4] he concluded that as far as Briton and Boer were then concerned:

There is the fusion of the races, an ideal if not practical necessity. There seems little reason to fear any future disruption, for on the material side the Dutch interests are ours. . . . The Dutch have their own ideals, different from ours, but not incompatible with complete political union. An attempt to do violence to their own ideals, or any hasty and unconsidered imposition of unsuitable English forms, will throw back the work of spiritual incorporation. . . . They have a strong church and a strong creed, certain educational ideas and social institutions which must long remain powers in the land. And let us remember that any South African civilization must grow up on the soil, and it must borrow from the Dutch race, else it is not true growth but a frail exotic. It will borrow English principles but not English institutions, since, while principles are grafts from human needs, institutions are the incrusted mosses of time which do not bear transplanting. It is idle to talk of universities such as Oxford, or public schools like Winchester, and any attempt to tend such alien plants will be a waste of money and time. South Africa will create her own nurseries, and on very different lines.

[1] London, Macmillan, 1897.
[2] London, Hutchinson, 1893.
[3] London, Fisher Unwin, 1923: New York, Stokes, 1923.
[4] Edinburgh, Blackwood, 1903.

Unfortunately, young Buchan's advice was not followed and, as he foresaw, the hostility of Milner to Afrikaans and the close adherence in education to British forms led to strong Afrikaans-speaking institutions such as Stellenbosch, with which every South African Prime Minister has been associated.

Despite the paternalism common to the times, Buchan's *Prester John*[1] anticipated the strong reaction of African leaders educated abroad but returning home with no suitable place in South African society; the breakaway tendencies of African churches and the long-range influence of American Negroes upon African nationalism in the Republic. No wonder that Buchan's biographer, Janet Adam Smith, reports in her: *A Biography*[2] that Jomo Kenyatta read *Prester John* in his prison days.

Winston Churchill, the last of the early observers we will note, made some remarkably sage predictions about East Africa, but his considerable South African writings focused on war. The young red-haired officer, who at one stage escaped from a Pretoria prison, gives a flash of his later style when he proclaims in *Ian Hamilton's March*[3] how:

By the unbroken success of his strategy Lord Roberts laid the Boer Republics low. We had taken possession of the Rand, the bowels whence the hostile government drew nourishment in gold and munitions of war. We had seized the heart of Bloemfontein, the brain at Pretoria. The greater part of the railways, the veins and nerves, that is to say, was in our hands. Yet, though mortally injured, the trunk still quivered convulsively, particularly the left leg, which, being heavily booted, had already struck us several painful and unexpected blows.

But Churchill at the time showed little insight into either Afrikaner or African character and aspirations.

In turning first to accounts of Afrikaner nationalism and then to African sources, it is important to note that Afrikaner historiography has improved immeasurably in recent years, with the definitive studies of P. J. van der Merwe, H. B. Thom, and D. W. Kruger, and F. A.

---

[1] London, Nelson, 1910.
[2] London, Hart-Davis, 1965: Boston, Little, Brown, 1966.
[3] London, Longmans, 1900.

van Jaarsveld's firm grasp of the flow of Afrikaner history in *The Afrikaner's Interpretation of South African History*.[1]

South Africa has produced relatively little overall political analysis. The author once chaired a session of a Natal University social science research conference where none of the hundred-odd South African participants classified himself as a political analyst. Both Afrikaner and African writers tend to drown in their own polemics, although neither group lacks intensely politically conscious individuals.

The Awakening of Afrikaner Nationalism 1868–1881, by Professor F. A. van Jaarsveld,[2] is an excellent background for the Afrikaner portions of this book. A history of the Cape National Party with a myriad of detail but without the same objectivity and careful selectivity is political correspondent Jan J. van Rooyen's *Die Nasionale Party: Sy Opkoms en Oorwinning-Kaapland se Aaandeel*, published by the Chief Council of the Cape National Party in 1956. Captain J. J. McCord's *South African Struggle*[3] is a strident defence of Afrikaner nationalism and attacks on the British government and multi-racialism by an English-speaking South African. Far more scholarly and unsympathetic is Sheila Patterson's *The Last Trek: A Study of the Boer People and the Afrikaner Nation*.[4] It is an historical and sociological description of the 'Boer or Afrikaner nation' since 1657, laying particular emphasis on concepts of being a 'chosen people', the raising of children and their education, and the social structure and cultural life of the Afrikaners.

The period of the Second World War and role of Afrikaner nationalism is documented in a hostile account by Michael Roberts and A. E. G. Trollip, *The South African Opposition 1939–1945*.[5] The early years of Nationalist rule are voluminously detailed in Gwendolen M. Carter's *The Politics of Inequality: South Africa Since 1948*.[6] The bitterest polemic against Afrikaner nationalism is *The Rise of the South African Reich* by Brian Bunting.[7] Penguin describes the author as 'a journalist in London', although some readers might have welcomed the

---

[1] Cape Town, Simondium, 1964.
[2] Cape Town, Human and Rosseau, 1961.
[3] Pretoria, De Bussy, 1952.
[4] London, Routledge & Kegan Paul, 1957.
[5] London, Longmans, Green, 1947.
[6] New York, Praeger, 1958: London, Thames & Hudson, 1958.
[7] London, Penguin, 1964.

fuller explanation of his being a Tass correspondent and for decades one of the top leaders of the Communist Party in South Africa.

The longest study of Afrikanerdom, *White Laager: The Rise of Afrikaner Nationalism*, by American professor William H. Vatcher, Jr.,[1] sees the decline of Afrikaner nationalism as inevitable, now hemmed into a traditional *laager* or circle of covered wagons in defence against the Africans. The French author, Paul Ginewski, writes on the *Bantustans*[2] with the more optimistic sub-title of 'A Trek Towards the Future'. The British political scientist, Christopher R. Hill, has also taken the title *Bantustans*,[3] viewing them in his sub-title as 'The Fragmentation of South Africa', and concluding that no matter how sincere white South Africans may be, this course is bound to fail.

Books on Bantustans, of which there are more, are a bibliographic bridge between Afrikaner and African nationalisms, since they are concerned with African territories, but as originally conceived by Afrikaners. *The Dynamics of the African National Congress*,[4] by Edward Feit, is the best description of that organization. Mary Benson's *The African Patriots: The Story of the African National Congress*[5] is frankly partisan, with warm sympathy for individuals and a glossing over of difficult issues. Albert Luthuli's *Let My People Go: An Autobiography*[6] is helpful for the emotional feel of the militant African *élite* but is more an appeal to British and American readers than a candid story of his life. The strong historical thread of Communism within the African nationalist movement is seen in Edward Roux's political history, *Time Longer Than Rope: A History of the Black Man's Struggle for Freedom in South Africa*.[7] Leo Kuper's *Passive Resistance in South Africa*[8] describes the 1952 campaign of the African National Congress and the South African Indian Congress. Kuper's *An African Bourgeoisie*[9] is an analytical study of the upper occupational categories in African society:

[1] New York, Praeger, 1965: London, Pall Mall, 1965.
[2] English translation: Cape Town, Human and Rousseau, 1961.
[3] London, Oxford University Press for Institute of Race Relations, 1964.
[4] London, Oxford University Press for Institute of Race Relations, 1962.
[5] London, Faber, 1963.
[6] London, Collins, 1962.
[7] London, Gollancz, 1948.
[8] New Haven and London, Yale, 1957.
[9] New Haven and London, Yale, 1965.

Kuper sees this *élite* as having an evolutionary impact by raising the colour-bar; or revolutionary, if it is 'thrown back on the African masses'.

The written record by Africans of the Republic is limited for the most part to political pamphlets and fiction. The author's library contains hundreds of political pamphlets and ephemera of African nationalism, too numerous to enumerate but having great collective significance. The publications of I. B. Tabata for the All-African Convention, B. M. Kies's work for the 'Anti-C.A.D.', and the co-writings of Tabata and Kies, published by the Non-European Unity Movement, are essential for a period when ideological issues were paramount. Newspapers and periodicals are critical to most studies of nationalism, but they are particularly important for African nationalism in South Africa because of the general paucity of books.

Novelist Peter Abrahams has attempted an African interpretation of such periods as the Great Trek in some of his novels but they are little help in a study of nationalism except in suggesting a deeply felt African emotion. The Westernized *milieu* of some African families against which much of African nationalism has taken place is best suggested in the biographical account *Drawn in Colour*[1] by Noni Jabavu, whose reaction to African life at that time in Uganda has made this book vastly unpopular among East Africans and West Africans, but this is characteristic of attitudes held by many Africans from the Republic and of the hostile reactions by other Africans.

One of the few Africans to essay African history in the Republic is S. M. Molema. His *The Bantu, Past and Present: An Ethnographical and Historical Study of The Native Races of South Africa*[2] corrected some contemporary white distortions of the African past. More political and covering the antecedents of the current nationalisms is his *Chief Moroka*.[3]

Jordan Ngubane analyses in *An African Explains Apartheid*[4] from the viewpoint of an African liberal. He describes the roots of Afrikaner nationalism, the conflict of the African National Congress and the Pan

[1] London, Murray, 1960.
[2] Edinburgh, W. Green, 1920.
[3] Cape Town, Methodist Publishing House, 1951.
[4] New York, Praeger, 1963: London, Pall Mall, 1963.

Africanist Congress, the complicating factor of Communism, and his own alternative to *apartheid*. Ngubane is one of the few critics of South African policy who attempts a non-vindictive and even compassionate view of the whites in his future society. Significantly, Ngubane's book has had very little impact. It is too radical a reorientation for most whites and not nearly radical enough for most white and black opponents of the South African government. His observation that 'to reach the top the Communist has to fight the Afrikaner nationalist, seek to destroy the capitalist in the United Party, undermine the Liberal, and sabotage the African nationalist', has not been well received by the anti-South African forces who endeavour to gloss over the Communist role and to seek a popular front. Since publication of his book, Ngubane has virtually sunk from sight. When the author had dinner with him in Swaziland in late 1965, Ngubane gave the impression, and partly confirmed it in his own words, that the intellectual isolation of his life in Swaziland, his disillusionment with some of the whites who were with him when he was Vice-President of the Liberal Party, ill health, and his lack of influence within and without the Republic have left him a shadow of his former self.

This study of *Afrikaner and African Nationalism* is concerned with the history of South Africa and with describing contemporary politics. Its specific purpose is a comparative interpretation starting from the significant roots and leading up to the two nationalisms at present. It is the political explanation for the sociological pattern of soil erosion in the reserves and soul erosion in the cities as white and black come into contact and conflict as portrayed in Alan Paton's *Cry, the Beloved Country*.[1] The same sociological theme runs through the beautifully written but overlooked Afrikaans novel of the same period by Frans Venter. Paton, in his superbly written biography of *Hofmeyr*[2], covers much of the same period as this study but with a different focus. Paton sees the tragedy of South Africa as the failure of English liberalism, the staunchest advocates of which have always been anglicized Afrikaners, to provide light and leadership towards a non-racial democracy.

One thesis underlying this current study is that English liberalism never really had more than a passing chance between the more power-

---

[1] London, Cape, 1948: New York, Scribner's, 1948.
[2] London, Oxford University Press, 1965.

B

ful and dynamic forces of Afrikaner and African nationalisms, although 'English' South Africans may well have a critical role to play tomorrow. The basic interaction today is Afrikaner and African.

The general American view of South Africa is through the eyes of liberal South Africans, reinforced by the history of American race relations. The conclusion is quickly drawn that if the United States is a melting pot, South Africa must be a pressure cooker. This may be, but the deeper forces at work in South Africa – Afrikaner and African – are far too complex to be easily resolved by the kind of alchemy Americans often assume they have developed to transmute hate into harmony.

CHAPTER I

THE TWO NATIONALISMS

Nationalism in South Africa is the subject of this book, but what do we mean when we speak of a South African nation? The original inhabitants – Strandlopers, Hottentots, Bushmen – have died out or are approaching extinction through absorption. South Africa for all practical purposes is peopled by comparatively recently adopted children. Although the most recent evidence suggests that there were some Bantu-speaking people in the northern Transvaal as early as A.D. 1000, the main Bantu wave came much later. By the middle of the seventeenth century, their camps and villages were found in more than one-half of South Africa. The progenitors of the Afrikaners came from the Netherlands, taking the western Cape and later joining the British to halt the advancing Africans and still later to subjugate most of them. The first British contingents arrived in the first half of the nineteenth century and the Indians in the second half. The Coloured (mixed) community is in a measure representative of the indigenous groups. It usually lacks cohesion and sometimes reveals a national rather than a nationalistic attitude.

If South Africa is not a nation, it does contain two powerful and competing nationalisms – African (about 12,000,000 people) and Afrikaner (about 2,000,000) – revolving around each other like a binary star and far outshining the weak light of a nebulous South African nationalism. Thus not South African but Afrikaner and African nationalisms overshadow the country. Significantly, the man in the street – black, brown, or white – is familiar with the term 'nation', although not as used in this book. The Afrikaner habit of speaking of *ons nasie* (our nation) to mean Afrikanerdom is recognized by other groups. Likewise, the concept of a Zulu 'nation' ('*umhlobo*') is widely accepted. There is no concept of an African nation in South Africa, a subject we will return to, but there has been a strong sense of African nationalism. These Afrikaner and African nationalisms inside the same borders show remarkable parallels in their form and provide a unique opportunity for comparative study.

Our framework for consideration of the two nationalisms assumes a three-phase development. Their separate characteristics will be discussed in detail for Afrikaner and African nationalisms. In general, phase one nationalism contains a very broad ideological spectrum with an emphasis on charismatic leadership; phase two sees an extension of the nationalism first held by the *élite* to a broader base, a greater emphasis upon economic issues within a growing class structure despite high social mobility; and in the third phase there is high national identification, professionalized political parties, and a greater concern for external relations with other nations.

The first significant stirrings of African nationalism followed the emergence of Afrikaner nationalism by about a century. Although African nationalism is only at the beginning of its intermediate, developmental phase, its time-lag behind Afrikaner nationalism has now shortened to about thirty years. After 1910, Afrikaners were allowed a peaceful if difficult path and came to political power at the close of the intermediate phase of their nationalism. African emergence will come nearer the middle of the intermediate phase. If external forces did not appear to dominate South Africa's future, one might venture to predict that an African break-through would require at least a decade in the white sphere; as it is, their political participation has begun in one form in the limited powers of the Transkei 'parliament', the first African 'reserve' which has under National Party ideology been transformed into a 'self-governing' Bantu state.

Afrikaner nationalism is today in its final phase, although the process of full maturation of this nationalism has been warped by the threat of destruction.

It is not surprising that Afrikaner and African nationalisms are uncompleted. Africa is the last of the great continents to make either a peaceful or a revolutionary transition from colonialism to nationalism. Prime Minister Harold Macmillan, in his famous 'Winds of Change' speech, delivered in Cape Town in early 1960, told the Afrikaner M.P.s that 'in the history of our times yours will be recorded as the first of the African nationalisms'. Most Afrikaners are rightly

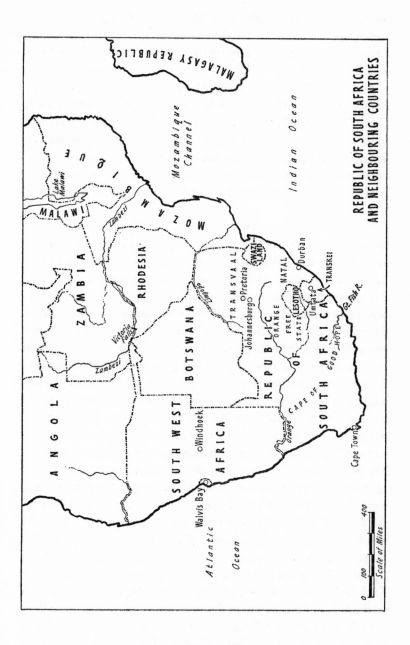

MALAGASY REPUBLIC

Mozambique Channel

Indian Ocean

Lake Malawi

MALAWI

Zambezi

ZAMBIA

RHODESIA

MOZAMBIQUE

ANGOLA

Victoria Falls

Zambezi

SOUTH WEST AFRICA

BOTSWANA

Limpopo

TRANSVAAL

SWAZI-LAND

Pretoria

Johannesburg

ORANGE FREE STATE

NATAL

Durban

REPUBLIC OF SOUTH AFRICA

LESOTHO

Umtata

TRANSKEI

Gt. Fish R.

CAPE OF GOOD HOPE

Orange

Windhoek

Walvis Bay

Cape Town

Atlantic Ocean

REPUBLIC OF SOUTH AFRICA
AND NEIGHBOURING COUNTRIES

Scale of Miles
0   100   400

proud of this. In the words of *Die Burger*, the Afrikaners 'opened the anti-colonialist century with their freedom struggle against British Colonialism and with that they set the example for colonial peoples all over the world'.

Anti-colonialism, the seed of Afrikaner nationalism, has a long history in South Africa. The early Boers (the Dutch word meaning 'farmer') who rebelled against the tyrannical rule of the Dutch East India Company's Governor in the eighteenth century were the first anti-colonialists south of the Sahara. Although Ethiopia has been autonomous for centuries, and Liberia was founded as an independent state in 1847, the first African country actually to free itself of colonial rule was South Africa.

In their famous 'Great Trek' of 1836, many of the Afrikaners trekked to the interior away from British rule. In 1843, the Transvaal *Voortrekkers* declared their independence; and in 1852 the independence of the Transvaal was recognized by the British government. The 1858 Republican constitution stipulated *inter alia* that there would be 'no equality between coloured people and the white inhabitants, either in *Church or in State*' (italics in original text). The Orange Free State was granted independence in 1854. The first Transvaal war was fought after the British forcibly occupied the country in 1877, and ended with Transvaal independence in 1881. In sympathy, a *taal* or Afrikaans language movement sprang up during the late nineteenth century in the intellectually more advanced British Cape Colony. Van Jaarsveld recognizes the role of eighteenth-century patriots and politically conscious Afrikaners in the nineteenth century, but no 'Afrikaner nationalism' before 1876. The defeat of the Boer commandos between 1899 and 1902 led to the constitution of South Africa in 1910. The powder horn, symbolic of the early *Voortrekkers*, is retained today as the emblem of the National Party. Afrikaner nationalism became full-blown in the new Union when the political nationalism of the north was extended to the south and wedded to the cultural nationalism flourishing there.

The Union was at first carried forward on a wave of sentiment for English–Afrikaans unity – 'two oxen in one yoke, drawing the wagon up the hill'. In the forefront of the 'conciliation' move were great Boer generals like Botha and Smuts. The British had shrewdly agreed that Botha should be the first Prime Minister of the Union. But in 1914

General J. B. M. Hertzog raised the banner of separate Afrikaner nationalism by founding the National Party. This party has been for more than half a century the vehicle of Afrikaner nationalism which carried it to ultimate final victory in the regaining of republican independence in 1961, not only for the two small Boer republics, but for the whole of South Africa – indeed a spectacular triumph after having been ground into the dust sixty years before.

Immediately after the Boer War, Afrikaner nationalism was hanging by a thread. The nation was defeated and impoverished by what the Afrikaners describe as the 'scorched earth policy of the British'. The language struggle was taken up, however, and the Afrikaners managed to maintain schools with funds from Holland, in which the Dutch language was taught. The Constitution of 1910 guaranteed equal language rights for English and Dutch. This important concession, secured by General Hertzog, became the life-blood of the nationalist movement – much to the amazement of the English element, which regarded Dutch as a dead language anyway. From it, however, sprang a virile tongue, Afrikaans, and a year after General Hertzog came to power in 1924, his Minister of the Interior, Dr. D. F. Malan, pushed through an amendment to the Constitution, declaring Afrikaans an official language of the Union. Dutch was also retained, but was in practice entirely supplanted by Afrikaans. Although *Die Volkstem* and *Die Land* preceded it, the first daily newspaper fighting the Afrikaner nationalist cause was founded in Cape Town in 1915, called *Die Burger*. It also started in Dutch, but in course of time became entirely Afrikaans. The first editor of this influential newspaper was Dr. D. F. Malan, who in 1948 achieved the great political triumph of leading a purely Afrikaner party to victory at the polls. General Hertzog's party had the assistance of English-speaking Labourites.

Afrikaner nationalists, like others in this century, soon realized that political independence does not satisfy nationalist aspirations if the symbols of the state are alien and economic control remains in foreign hands. Thus there was the bitter and successful struggle for Dutch, and later Afrikaans, language rights from 1905 until 1925, the fight for a co-equal South African flag, won in 1928, leading to the eventual disappearance of the Union Jack in 1958, and the battle for the republican status won on 31 May 1961. The fight goes on for Afrikaner 'equality' under the present 80 per cent South African English and foreign economic control. There are separate Afrikaans banks, insurance companies, savings societies, and co-operatives, just as the cultural side is also set apart with Afrikaans universities and Afrikaans versions of the Red Cross (*Noodhulpliga*) and Boy Scouts (*Voortrekkers*). In the communications field the battle of Afrikaner versus English is carried into the linguistically segregated newspapers, magazines, and broadcasting.

The right of self-determination in South Africa has been a consistently successful rallying cry for enlisting foreign support. The Boers and the latter-day Afrikaners – a majority of the white population – had enjoyed the spiritual support of most of the world in the struggle against British colonialism. Subscription lists were filled in Boston and Baltimore for the Boers, and Boer sympathies divided the British people. A prevailing American view of 1902 was summed up in the words of eight-year-old Allen Dulles, who was to head the Central Intelligence Agency, in a publication which attracted the attention of his uncle, Secretary of State Lansing, and of President Theodore Roosevelt. Young Dulles interviewed Boer representatives and concluded:

> The Boers are very industrious and are hard workers and are very fond of the Bible, but the Boer prisoners are not even allowed to have the Psalms for they think it will incurage [*sic*] them. They love their country especially and they ought to have it in spite of the wicked English who are trying to rob them of it. I hope that the Boers will win for the Boers are in the wright [*sic*] and the British are wrong in the War.

Half a century later the African people of the Republic have the spiritual support of Americans and most United Kingdom citizens. Afrikaners who once profited from foreign sympathy are assailed on the same principles as they, in their turn, are said by Marquard and others to have become a colonial power inside South Africa.

Before Afrikaners gained even their first goal of language rights, the African National Congress in 1912 had been formed to begin its uncompleted struggle for political rights similar to those the Afrikaners had wrung from the British and their descendants within South Africa. Bantu tribes had engaged in many wars, some successful but most of them not, in resistance against the gradual subjugation of the country east and north of the Fish River. There had been political groupings involving more than one tribe but none taking in Africans throughout the Union. Gradually the Bantu drifted to towns looking for work – usually the poorest-paid and most unattractive jobs. Significantly, an early labour strike stemmed from the urbanization of Africans of various tribes on the Witwatersrand and the menial work assigned to them. In 1918, when most of Johannesburg lacked a water-borne sewage system, African sanitary workers 'downed buckets' and demanded sixpence a day more. The strike was linked to the new African National Congress and its demands for political change, loosely described as socialism, and was broken by imprisoning the leaders and using African police as labourers. Although its leaders were from time to time charged with specific offences, the A.N.C. as an organization was not banned until 1960.

In the 1920s Clements Kadalie, a remarkable Nyasaland African, organized African workers on a large scale in the International Commercial Workers Union and pressed for higher wages. The African National Congress led innumerable protests and continued pre-eminent in African politics until it began sharing leadership in 1960 with the Pan Africanist Congress, organized in 1958 principally by defecting A.N.C. members. Both these branches of African Nationalism continue to push for political rights. While they were legal, they had the great majority of urban Africans behind them. At his peak, as leader of the African National Congress, Luthuli claimed 150,000 to 250,000 supporters, or about 2 to 3 per cent of the Bantu population. How many of the rest would have chosen him or their traditional and more conservative leaders is open to debate. The A.N.C./P.A.C. strength in South Africa is difficult to measure today, as they have been banned since 1960. They certainly retain substantial overseas support.

Both of the intertwined nationalisms have grown out of a deep sense of pride, both spurred on by deep humiliation, and both finding outside world sympathy in their initial stages of development. South Africa's weakness, rooted in its lack of a single unifying nationalism, sets it apart from most European and Afro-Asian countries. Although South Africa is part of a tropical continent, the climate is temperate; although Africa is undeveloped, South Africa has a complex economy, already, for instance, exporting steel to the United States. African nationalism emerging in such an environment is akin to nationalism in underdeveloped parts of the world, while Afrikaner nationalism has had more in common with nationalism in Europe. Afrikaans resembles Norwegian in that the language was promoted as distinct from the prevailing languages (Dutch and English on the one hand and Danish on the other) as an expression of political nationalism. African nationalism in the Republic transcends different linguistic groups for which a common language (such as Hindi in India) has not evolved. The language of African nationalism in South Africa is at present English, just as the languages of nationalism through most of the sub-Sahara are English and French.

We have described the existence of two nationalisms within the same geographical country, and now turn to the lack of a strong overriding nationalism before taking up the non-nationalists.

CHAPTER II

THE LACK OF UNITY AND THE ABSENCE OF SYMBOLS OF A SINGLE NATIONALISM

There are no universal symbols of even a tenuous South African nationalism. The symbols so important in nineteenth-century European nationalism or twentieth-century African nationalism are restricted to particular groups. Even before the Crown disappeared with the advent of a republic, it had carried little weight with Afrikaners. They demonstrated their war-time dislike of Britain by refusing to stand in cinemas for 'God Save the King', which Afrikaners felt was played far more frequently in South Africa than in the United Kingdom for its propaganda value. Occasionally their rude rush for the exit provoked a free-for-all fight with those who regarded it as a sacred hymn. Today the anthem is *'Die Stem'* ('The Call') – one of the better-written and most moving of national anthems – but its historical allusions to the creak of the trekker ox-wagons have deep meaning only for the Afrikaner. When Afrikaners sing *'ons sal offer wat jy vra'* ('we shall give what you ask') and 'live and die for South Africa', the meaning is only for the Afrikaner nation. One has only to hear it sung by Afrikaners in Afrikaans and then on a very rare occasion by the 'English' in English to know the tremendous emotional difference. There is now, however, a growing number of 'English' who do sing the anthem in Afrikaans with a sentiment approaching that of the Afrikaner. The foregoing is not to imply that South Africans of British stock do not love their country and have not willingly risked their lives and died for it on the battlefield, but *'Die Stem'* has lesser meaning. Neither 'God Save the Queen' nor *'Die Stem'* have deep emotional significance for the African population. All the African sub-groups recognize *'Nkosi Sikilel'i Afrika'* 'God Bless Africa' – not God

Bless *South* Africa – as their anthem, though it is sung in different tribal languages.

Another indication of the lack of corporate South African nationalism is that despite a few great fortunes made in the country, there are almost no great philanthropists. Universities, art galleries, libraries, and research of all kinds cry out for assistance, but few significant bequests have been made. Cecil John Rhodes was pre-Union English and scarcely counts. The wealthiest South African magnate, Sir Ernest Oppenheimer, died without leaving a substantial charitable bequest, although his wise son made large gifts in his father's name. The sons and grandsons of such earlier mining magnates as Abe Bailey and J. B. Robinson show a deep concern for South Africa. Substantial numbers of Afrikaners are worth half a million dollars, but their wealth is tied up in land and has not been easily divisible without handicapping the new generation. On the whole, Afrikaners have become rich too recently perhaps, and Africans not at all, to encourage the expectations of giving on a truly national scale. Even though there are some benefactions by individuals on a country-wide basis, the narrower appeal of the group to which the donor belongs far outruns any sense of general South Africanism.

Military policy, too, responds to ethnic particularism. Official defence policy shifted from 1960 to 1965 to a concentration upon internal rather than external dangers. Then, with greater internal security, it began swinging back to an external focus. The lack of a South African nationalism was implicitly recognized in 1960 by the government when it pushed the organization of voluntary commandos (a Boer War term) largely among the Afrikaans-speaking whites. This changed later, and when Defence Minister Fouche retired from the post in 1966, the English-language press praised him for his fairness as between the two white language groups. The shift to internal concern was evidenced when Centurion tanks were sold to Switzerland while armoured cars were bought from Britain and sub-machine guns from Belgium. These measures marked a change in the government estimate as to which of the country's citizens would defend it in time of war. In the First World War thousands of Africans performed manual labour in France as members of the 'Native Corps', and the Cape Coloured Corps did transport work. In the Second World War the Cape Corps continued and, in practice, its soldiers in North Africa were armed, although no Africans from South Africa were armed to oppose Hitlerian racialism. General Smuts had 25,000 Zulus trained to fight an invasion, but they were never used. A 'whites only' policy prevailed in the defence forces even though the forces were expanded rapidly after 1960. Recently a return was made to limited Coloured recruitment for segregated Army units and the Navy. This successive narrowing of the categories of dependable soldiers is obviously a function of potential disloyalty. It also has a striking counterpart in the attitude towards treason. On the other hand, one must point out that South Africa is policed by a smaller force than that of New York City, and that a majority of the police in South Africa are Africans! Most of them are in the ranks, although by 1966 a number of Africans had become station commanders in 'non-white' areas.

The concept, so prevalent in other countries, of a common nationalism, is, as we have initially noted, absent in South Africa. The loose fabric of South African nationalism is evident in the handling of treason charges. In law, treason is a crime punishable by death. In practice, it draws a lesser punishment than rape. When *English-speaking whites* failed to shoot their way into Johannesburg and capture political control in the Jameson Raid of 1896, old Paul Kruger said the prisoners taken in the ill-fated adventure would be shot. But magnanimity won the day and they were nearly all out of jail in a few months. When *Afrikaners* took up arms against the state in the 1914 Rebellion and killed government soldiers, most of them were freed within a few weeks. Some, including the famous Boer leader General De Wet, were sentenced to a few years' imprisonment. When *Africans* were on trial for treason in Pretoria during the period 1956 to 1961, it was clear that even if they were not acquitted, their sentence would not have been hanging but a few years in jail. This goes so deep into South African consciousness that in the Second World War, when a famous South African boxer, Robey Leibrandt, landed in South Africa from a German submarine to undertake sabotage, General Smuts told confidants than on no account was he to be shot as a traitor, lest this evoke Afrikaner memories of Jaap Fourie in *Die Rebellie*, or even echoes of British action at Slaagtersnek in the early days of British differences with the Boers. A number of African nationalists are today in prison rather than hung for crimes of sabotage lest they become martyrs. This weakness in penalties for treason suggests that either men do not feel the same loyalty towards South Africa as characterizes nationalism elsewhere, or that different governments are careful not to make martyrs.

Nationality as a symbolic concept in South Africa tends to be identified with love for one's immediate physical surroundings. To some it is, in the words of a South African of Scots descent, 'A challenge with all its conflicts and problems, and home with all the implications of "home".' But this feeling is limited. Thus many Cape Afrikaner, English, and Coloured people abroad may share a nostalgia for the Western Cape, and have been known to abandon successful careers to return to its extraordinary beauty and salubrious climate. Elsewhere in Africa, the longing for 'their' country by South African Africans often puzzles other Africans, for the latter fail to see a compatibility between a Zulu's antagonism to the laws of the country and his love for the cattle and hills of Zululand or his nostalgia for a smoky, rowdy *shebeen* (speakeasy or unlicensed bar) in an African township of Johannesburg.

The symbols of a single South Africa find their greatest expression outside the country. Thus to hear 'Natalians' (whites from the most 'English' province) speaking wretched Afrikaans in the London underground is to listen to either nostalgia for home or an almost pathetic search for a national symbol as they strain to set themselves apart from the British people around them. A Zulu or Afrikaans folksong or a 'Malay' dish sometimes provide a link among English, African, Coloured and Afrikaner South Africans in a foreign land and a sense of comradeship virtually impossible to duplicate within the borders of the country. When the Springboks (a springbok is the symbol of South African white sporting teams) play abroad, there is fairly wide national support among all sports fans. But when the Springboks have played Britain or New Zealand in South Africa, the African and Coloured fans have rooted wildly for the visitors and thrown bottles at the South African players, and are now barred from Bloemfontein stadium. Conversely, white citizens take a sporting pride in the accomplishments of African (South African) boxers in overseas rings, but not when matched with a white boxer in an adjacent country. Even serious discussions of South Africa's problems and prospects are more often and more easily carried out abroad, if they involve people who are at political odds within the Republic.

The blooming of South African nationalism abroad while wilting at home was most marked in the Second World War. The reason, as expressed to the author by a prominent Afrikaner, stemmed from:

... the almost traumatic shock to the Afrikaners, including General Hertzog, when South Africa, under Smuts' leadership, declared war in 1939 instead of staying out like every non-British independent country, including America, Holland, etc. The whole thing was to us a denial of our independence and a reassertion of British imperialism.

Gangs of Afrikaners assaulted individual soldiers in uniform on the streets of Johannesburg. When a group of soldiers retaliated, one pitched battle with rocks was only quelled by the use of troops. Yet in North Africa, where 50 per cent of the South Africans were Afrikaners, a real comradeship was forged in the face of Rommel's legions. (The figure is generally given in books as 60 per cent Afrikaners, but this was a war-time propaganda gimmick put out to secure Afrikaner support.) Towards the end of the war a number of 'poor white' Afrikaners also joined up to serve on the home-front for the financial return. The leadership of professional Afrikaner generals such as Dan Pienaar was outstanding. Thousands of English and Afrikaners returned home after V.E.-Day determined to keep their battle-worn unity and to tackle the looming racial problem of their country.

This new spirit faltered when the home-front passed insensitively over the valour of the all-volunteer troops and turned to renewed peace-time commerce. The disgruntled soldiers may even have provided the narrow margin of victory for Dr. Malan's National Party, just five scant years after it had been crushed on an end-the-Hitler-war platform in 1943. The war-time spirit of co-operation did give birth to the Torch Commando led by 'Sailor' Malan, an R.A.F. fighter ace. But the Commando ran into differences over the role of Coloured ex-servicemen. Their exclusion diluted the moral basis of the movement, leaving it an auxiliary of the predominantly 'English' United Party.

The famous leader of the United Party, Prime Minister Jan Christian Smuts, allowed party hacks to block the entry of the ablest ex-servicemen into politics, and thus added to his reputation of surrounding himself with 'yes men'. A decade later, in 1958, the United Party did try unsuccessfully to enlist the support of the 'veteran group', whose businesses and families were by then in the mid-stream of life.

Finally, the English and Afrikaans war comrades found themselves enmeshed in the long-established division of their respective language groups, a split accentuated by bitter divisions at home during the war. Many men of both groups have described in comments to the author how they drifted away from a common loyalty as they re-absorbed the attitudes of their own section. The unity of these white South Africans as a veteran group was not again approached until the broad white unity felt during the Rhodesian crisis and criticism over South West Africa. The shock of the Sharpeville upheaval of 1960 did stagger both white sections, but both of them rallied so quickly that no new unity was born. Whereas most educated Africans had supported Smuts in the war against Hitler Germany because of the publicity given to various racialistic statements by the Nazi leader, after Sharpeville it was only the Coloured community who rallied to the white leadership. It is notable that many promises by Nationalist politicians to the Coloured that they would be 'rewarded' for their 'loyalty' led to a sour feeling among many Coloureds after 1961, when the hoped-for changes in discriminatory laws did not come about.

The economic boom of South Africa in the decades after the Second World War has meant that the kind of testing a depression can provide has not been given. More than one observer has expressed doubts as to whether even the Afrikaner himself will retain his loyalty to his people in time of crisis. Has the Afrikaner been caught up in materialism to a point where under pressure he would, in de Kiewiet's pithy phrase, waver in his choice of the *volk* or the *volkswagen*?

Few Afrikaners have doubts but that the *volk* would be the choice. A few years ago, English-speaking South Africans would have clearly chosen the automobile over politics. Today, they are divided in large part because of what they consider to be the unfair and hypocritical statements and actions of the United Kingdom and the United States and most of all by the United Nations, spurred by the African states. If there is no universal symbol of nationalism for all the people of South Africa, and even a lack of a common symbol for all the white section, there is a large measure of agreement on the wrongness of the acts of the outside world. A few years ago it would have been unthinkable that Sir de Villiers Graaff as leader of the United Party would have expressed support for Prime Minister Ian Smith in the weeks after the Rhodesian's Unilateral Declaration of Independence. If all the whites, and especially the 'English', are not enthusiastic about the *volk*, it is not a contradiction to say that the vast majority of the whites resent foreign detractors of the Republic.

On the economic front there is a common unity of purpose among the whites. But as Professor L. H. Samuels writes: 'In the Republic of South Africa there is not one economic and social system, but at least two.'[1] Many Africans are part of the modern economic system along with all the whites and do share certain economic goals, but loyalty and identification are to the individual corporation or employer and not to an economic system as a whole with which they can identify.

South African nationalism is limited for the most part to the formal concepts of citizenship. All citizens carry the same passport and are subject to laws passed by the same parliament even though such legislation may not apply equally to all citizens. Although there is a cultural similarity in the dress and many of the food-habits of the middle-class Africans, Afrikaners, and English, they themselves do not recognize the similarity nor appreciate it when it is pointed out.

South Africa did, however, approach national feeling inside the country as never before when the then Prime Minister Hendrik Verwoerd went to London, in March 1961, for the Commonwealth Conference. A thin pro-Commonwealth unity bound the two white groups, and included a majority of the Coloured and Asians, as well as a minority of Africans. But the unity of the last three groups was based upon a feeling that *apartheid* was best attacked inside rather than outside the Commonwealth. In terms of individuals, it is probable that more persons in South Africa can be united in opposition to any conceivable government than is the case with any other country.

The great unifying agency of war against an outside danger has never come to forge a common South African loyalty. The two World Wars did not constitute an immediate danger and were primarily fought by the white groups. The Second World War led to

[1] *African Studies in Income and Wealth*, London, Bowes and Bowes, 1963, p. 162.

C

unprecedented community of feeling between English whites and the non-whites opposed to Hitler, but it did not include the Afrikaners. In contrast, that sower of disunity – civil war – plagued white–black relations for a long century, only to be succeeded by a white–white war whose seeds of hatred still bear unusually bitter fruit. But the generation of Afrikaners who remember the Boer War have had much of their hurt assuaged, while the British feel that a sense of grievance has been deliberately encouraged in succeeding generations as a device to foster Afrikaans unity. Some Afrikaners disagree and argue that the British left an 'occupation army' in the shape of a dominant British-minded settler population. This power had to be broken and finally was in the 1966 election. Previously, many Afrikaners felt there was always the chance that the British would regain power by using non-white allies, through the old Cape Native vote and Coloured votes.

This process embittered successive generations of Afrikaners, but it also helped bring success at the polls, until the political triumph was complete. A major step in the process of broadening symbols of nationalism for many Afrikaners was the establishment of the long-sought republic on 31 May 1961, following the referendum of the white population. The release from a narrow Afrikaner loyalty is evident in this private comment of a senior government official:

Just as the *Voortrekkers* gave way to the Boers (a broader group), and the Boers gave way to the Afrikaners (a still broader group), so now people like myself who think of ourselves as Afrikaners must lose our exclusiveness in a broader citizenship. I wrote my old father, who was born in the Orange Free State Republic and helped defend it in the Boer War, that an old book is closed and a new one opened. On polling day, I voted for the republic and for the dissolution of the National Party as we have known it.

This transfer of feeling does create an ambivalence in Afrikaners. As they lose a unified group feeling there is the tendency to project their symbols for all of white South Africa if not for all South Africa. Less and less does one find the flags of the old 'Boer Republic' displayed by the most enthusiastic nationalists, much as the Confederate flag was revived in the American South during the anti-integration manoeuvres after the Second World War. Cabinet Minister Jan de Klerk, who may be classified as among the more conservative Afrikaner nationalists, told the *Suid-Afrikaanse Akademie vir Wetenskap en Kuns* (South

African Academy for Science and Art) in Pochefstroom in 1965, that the national flag should be exhibited in all school halls, classrooms, and playgrounds, and should play a part in all school functions. The Minister warned that the change from an agrarian to an industrial society was producing a new type of Afrikaner whose culture was shallow. This Afrikaner found his own 'national identity' had become nothing more than a nuisance to him and he was unaware of dangers all around him. The Minister concluded with a call for a spiritual revival as against a materialistic emphasis and greater devotion to an emotional stimulus such as the 'national flag as a symbol of national feeling'.

While regretting the passing of the old sense of 'language purity' and strict Afrikaner nationalism, Minister de Klerk was at the same time calling for a new and broader loyalty to the South African flag. Young people who pledge total allegiance to that flag without the older National Party symbols can scarcely think as deeply of a different 'national identity' meaning Afrikanerdom. If the two concepts are not fully compatible, it is an indication of the transitional stage in which the Afrikaner, and also the Englishman without the Union Jack, finds himself.

That South Africa lacks a national symbol to unify it is obvious to the most casual visitor, but it is less evident what price South Africa pays in its divided front towards the world, expensive internal security, and an economic system in which many who labour consider it unjust. Few countries have ever been more lacking in universal symbols. Political differences in Italy, linguistic struggles in Belgium and Canada, labour versus management in the American depression, or the tribal antipathies in new African states, are all of a lesser order in that symbols to unify them have been or can be more easily developed.

CHAPTER III

THE NON-NATIONALISTS

If we look beyond Afrikaners and Africans, we find there are three important sub-groups below the threshold of nationalism in the Republic: the 1,300,000 white English-speaking people; the 1,500,000 predominantly Afrikaans-speaking Coloured community; and the 480,000 'Indian' group.

The English group cannot be described in simple, clear-cut terms – an indication of its commitment to South African, rather than sub-group, interests. This lack may also be taken rightly as a symbol of the bridge between Britain and English-speaking South Africans. In the past, the Union Castle Steamship line was a little like a ferryboat across the Irish Sea. 'English' nationalism in South Africa was not clearly differentiated from the nationalism in Great Britain. The only noteworthy English-speaking association on narrow political lines in the last decade was U.N.E.S.S.A. (United English-Speaking South Africans), a feeble organization led by an Irishman and linked to an ineffective revolutionary group. Its principal function was to issue strong statements on behalf of the English section, which were usually highly unrepresentative and served to infuriate the Afrikaners.

The tie with Britain had weakened after the Second World War when there was no longer wide support for the since defunct Dominion Party. In the view of many English-speaking South Africans, Britain was ill-advised to admit so many 'half-fledged and hostile black African states into the Commonwealth', as one South African expressed it. With the demise of the Dominion Party, the Sons of England, a patriotic organization, carries on but is likewise viewed as anachronistic by many local English. However, it has now pledged allegiance to the Republic and has good relations with the government. If the English nationalism is subconsciously diffused by a form of dual loyalty, it is also unheard in the strident noise of the market-place where most English energies are spent. With the principal exception of the eastern Cape and the plantations of Natal, the English farming community has disappeared or blended into the countryside. English South Africans in business are concentrated at the seaports of Cape Town, Port Elizabeth, and Durban, or in Johannesburg, the terminus of flights from Europe. In each instance, ties with Great Britain have been a matter of everyday practical importance, despite the loss of Commonwealth status in 1961.

The attitude of British-descended whites towards nationalism in general has gone through three phases. In the 1920s South Africa reflected some of the anti-nationalism and anti-patriotism prevalent in Great Britain and summed up in the famous Oxford-debate refusal to fight for king and country. This attitude was transmitted through South African newspaper editors, who were nearly all born in Great Britain, and through the English-language universities whose faculties were likewise drawn from 'home'. But still a sense of imperial mission remained stronger in those on the outposts of empire than in Britain.

In the 1930s the militant nationalism of Hitler and Mussolini repelled the South African British and caused their drawing closer to the United Kingdom. There was criticism of Afrikaner nationalism, but Dr. Malan's tiny group was then ineffective and the main proponent of Afrikaner nationalism, General Hertzog, had made his peace, in a sense, with General Smuts (for the English) by joining in the new United South African National Party in a process known as *same-smelting*. This 'smelting', as it was described politically, occurred in the crucible of the great depression.

The break-up of the Hertzog–Smuts alliance, in September 1939, unleashed the present Afrikaner nationalism, which in turn created a spirit of greater anti-Afrikaner feeling among the British-descended South Africans in the 1940s and 1950s. Thus a dislike of Afrikaner nationalism in general spiralled into a specific dislike of nationalisms in general.

This feeling explains why the 'English' in South Africa considered U.N.E.S.S.A. and its 'nationalistic' statements as 'cranky'. The spirit of the 'English' South Africans is not grouped around a central core of nationalism, but is identified with rather wide and elastic bonds. The resilience of these ties is proved by the remarkable cohesiveness of the

English-speaking section through eighteen years of Afrikaner Nationalist government. Despite incessant propaganda, the National Party had, until the 1966 election, gained only a small minority of 'English' votes and has depended upon the greater population growth of the Afrikaner section and upon recapturing Afrikaner *Sappe* (voters for Smuts's United South African National Party) to swell its political strength. However, it is probable from careful calculations that in 1966 the pro-Nationalist votes of English-speaking South Africans actually equalled the pro-United Party votes of the Afrikaans-speaking voters.

The respective sizes of the white voting groups have long threatened obliteration of an 'English' nationalism. To have formally solidified would have been to lose. Thus the 'English' have been tactical voters and have sacrificed the leadership of 'their party' to Afrikaners. They have compromised on one issue after another in seeking to split Afrikaner nationalism – successfully in the 1930s and so far unsuccessfully in the 1950s and 1960s. In the 1966 General Election, the United Party was by many criteria to the political right of the National Party, especially in its attitude towards Rhodesia and its own racialistic propaganda of '*swart gevaar*' towards Bantustans.

A natural reaction to this everlasting readiness for tactical compromise was a repudiation of the United Party by a significant minority and the formation of a more liberal Progressive Party under an Afrikaner leader but with largely English-speaking support, including many South Africans of Jewish background. Its supporters are less anti-Afrikaans in a cultural sense and more pro-African than the bulk of United Party supporters, especially in Natal. While it captured a dozen sitting M.P.s from the United Party, all but one were wiped out in the 1961 election. The one, Helen Suzman, was re-elected to parliament as a United Party-turned Progressive in the 1961 and 1966 elections from a rich white suburb of Johannesburg on a platform of merit, not colour, as the desired basis of the franchise. It was the first success of its kind in South African history. Farther to the left, such 'English' as Alan Paton and Patrick Duncan had earlier (in 1950) created a Liberal Party from all groups – a few Afrikaners but mostly 'English' and Africans.

The one province with a special 'English' feeling has always been Natal. Attitudes of Natalians towards other groups have gone through a fascinating series of shifts within the last decade. Traditionally, some of the strongest antipathies in South Africa have been those directed against the 'coolies' by white Natalians. Segregation in South Africa in modern times received its greatest impetus in Natal when the upward mobility of the Indians began a process of residential integration with the English. The 'pegging act' in Natal and General Smuts's strong support for it laid the corner-stone for the post-war *apartheid* policy within urban areas. Of all the cities in South Africa, Durban was the first to enthusiastically embrace the Group Areas Act setting up racial zones for the different population groups.

From the formation of South Africa until about 1958, the great enemy of the Natalian was the Indian. He was then succeeded by the Afrikaner in Natal eyes. This was the period of the Federal Party in Natal and all the manoeuvres towards secession of English-speaking Natal from the iniquitous Afrikaner-contaminated Union of South Africa. Anti-Afrikaner feeling culminated in the Republican referendum of 1960. Today the Afrikaner is embraced and indeed there is an unprecedented harmony and mutuality of feeling with the Indians as the third object of hate (or fear?) has arisen – the Zulu. All of this has coincided with the growing pro-Pretoria feeling and the movement away from loyalty to the United Kingdom. The latter was epitomized by the action of some English-speaking Durbanites when they hauled down a British flag in disgust when a tanker with oil for Rhodesia was driven off from Lourenço Marques by the British Navy and arrived in Durban. Although Prime Minister Verwoerd refused to let the tanker discharge in Durban, the anger of the crowd was directed against the Union Jack.

An English group-sense is also weakened by the feelings of the 103,000 members of the 'English group' who are of Jewish descent. Under the push of anti-Semitism in South Africa from both Afrikaner and English (which is still not nearly as strong as in the United States), fearing African rule, South African Jews support what is probably the strongest Zionism in the world. They have sent more money *per capita* to Israel than any Jewish group in the world – far exceeding the Americans – and a higher percentage of settlers have gone to Israel from South Africa than is the case of the United States and of other countries where Jews are relatively prosperous. In the days after South

Africa withdrew from the Commonwealth, the thought was frequently expressed by Jews that they might have to go to Israel. More recently, South African Jews have become more pro-South African and their protests were probably the cause of the replacement of one Israeli Ambassador in Pretoria following an Israeli action against South Africa at the United Nations.

In addition to the Jews, there is another white group which, although of Afrikaans descent, is socially, economically, and politically divorced from Afrikaner nationalism as the nationalists define it, and whose members are sometimes referred to as 'anglicized Afrikaners'. Although they speak English at home, the term is often resented. They claim to be South African and not Afrikaner or English, but the group has little cohesiveness. Some of them sing '*Die Stem*' as their national anthem, and others abhor it. They are South African in the absence of being anything else, but their position tends to be amorphous. Their only unity is in reaction to criticism.

Within the so-called 'Indian' community exists an understandable ambivalence. Since the days when a young lawyer named Mohandas Gandhi was arousing his people in Durban, the emotional tie with India has been kept firm by discrimination against Indians in South Africa. But divisions of loyalties between the land of their birth and the subcontinent of their origin have been fomented by the Hindu–Muslim split and by political differences between the South African Indian Congress and conservative Indian organizations.

Indian leaders meanwhile have sought to forge close bonds with African nationalists, but the Indian masses, many in daily competition with Zulus, have fearful memories of the worst rioting in the history of the country, when in 1949 Zulus murdered and raped them and pillaged the Indian areas of Durban. Their reaction in seeking the protection of Afrikaner policemen heightens the ambivalence. Only in the last few years has Afrikaner nationalism conceded that the Indian community has a permanent future in South Africa.

The 1,500,000 strong Coloured community, descended from Hottentots, Bushmen, Europeans, and 'Malay' slaves from Java, with more recent additions of newer European and Bantu 'genes', are a distinct and relatively stable community. They speak European languages (more Afrikaans than English), follow formal religions (more Christian than Muslim), and in the urban areas have achieved a middle-class personality. They fight against a national-group feeling because it runs contrary to their integration in the white community and they have fewer urges towards nationhood than any other major group. They tend to say, 'We belong to South Africa', as opposed to the more common cry, 'South Africa belongs to us'. At the same time, they find it relatively easy to accept the broader symbols of a South African nationalism. For example, 'God Save the Queen' and '*Die Stem*' are both sung on occasion, and neither rankles the masses. They willingly served South Africa in two World Wars and their veterans are proud of it. A few individual friendships in South Africa bridge the colour chasm, but perhaps the only group affection is between Cape Afrikaners and Cape Coloureds, who share a common history, and, for many, a common ancestry. The middle-class function in creating nationalism is supported by the fact that the Coloured community has the greatest intensity of class feeling as well as the strongest South African nationalism.

We can assess South African nationalism by quoting Lincoln's admonition in the Civil War President's first inaugural address: 'Though passion may have strained, it must not break the bonds of affection.' This kind of humanism has little meaning for all people in South Africa, because there is little affection for all people. The title of G. H. Calpin's book may have said it best: *There Are No South Africans.*[1] Even the English, Afrikaners, and some Coloured people who draw together against the *swart gevaar* (black danger) do so out of fear and not in mutual affection. This negative unity is even clearer when we look for positive symbols of nationalism.

[1] London, Thomas Nelson, 1941.

CHAPTER IV

CLASS AND NATIONALISM AMONG AFRIKANERS AND AFRICANS

Class in South Africa is often submerged in the waves of the binary nationalism. Ethnic groups substitute in part for class both in racial groups (European *v.* African) and in social/ cultural groups (English *v.* Afrikaner), where the English have tended in the past to form a superior class to the Afrikaners. Thus when class operates within Afrikanerdom, it is in a twice diluted strength.

Tribalism is less important among the more sophisticated Bantu population of the Republic when compared to tribal feelings in such a vigorous but diverse country as Nigeria. The greater urban concentration in South Africa, and the Westernization of Africans, have led to a more Western type of class structure within the urban areas. As we have said, the largely urban Coloured population displays a more easily identified upper-, middle- and lower-class structure than other ethnic groups. But in almost all situations, forces which would tend to develop and emphasize factors of class are secondary to the overriding political considerations.

Within the two nationalisms there is no serious challenge to the consensus that class and other sectarian loyalties be submitted to the national need. Afrikaner dogma thunders from a thousand platforms to maintain what former Prime Minister Strijdom called 'White Christian civilization'. This cry in turn is matched, as an overriding consideration for African nationalism, by a hatred of the very concept of colour as a determinate of civilization, and a resolve to grind it into the red dust of Africa. It is perhaps remarkable, and a tribute to a small handful of whites with different ideas from the Strijdoms, that relatively unsophisticated Africans make a distinction in their opposition to the laws of some whites from anti-whitism in general. However, from about 1961 there was a marked growth of African hatred for those people called in Xhosa *amaBhulu*, or Afrikaners. This was most marked in urban areas. There appears to have been some lessening of this antipathy in rural areas and possibly in the cities, although observers differ strongly, and the author finds wide differences of opinion on this among Africans in Cape Town and Johannesburg. Africans abroad are adamant in believing hatred is higher. Critics of government attribute any lessening of antipathy to censorship of critical views and the success of government propaganda and financial blandishments for chiefs and others.

The skewing of classes so that Afrikaners lack a normal-size lower class and Africans a normal-size upper and middle class means that the role of the upper class in importing foreign ideas (fascism, democracy, or Communism, for example) is of less importance within Afrikaner nationalism than in other countries. But the existence of two juxtaposed nationalisms means that the upper class of South Africa as a whole – the whites – does act unwittingly as the importer of ideas for consumption by the lower class as a whole – the Africans. Whereas, ironically, Afrikaners once leaped to import nationalistic ideas in their struggle against the foreign and local 'English', they now feel compelled to draw a curtain against such ideas and influence.

Class structure is of more marked significance to Afrikaner than to African nationalism. But divisive forces in both nationalisms rising out of the clash of interests are always relatively weak in the face of the powerful cohesive identification flowing from the clash of the two opposing nationalisms.

The transition of Afrikaners from an essentially rural people with their political strength embedded in *platteland* (prairie or rural) seats, to their present position after the trek to the cities, the loss of some 'tribal' *mores*, and equal dependence upon rural and urban worker constituencies, has not produced a visible conflict of interest within the ethnic group. Taxes are still arranged for the benefit of the farmer and, with the rapid rise in the value of old farms, special care has been taken to help farmers avoid heavy death duties. Petitions at National Party Congresses may raise the voice of the Nationalist consumer, but they can never be very loud without attracting criticism for dividing the *volk*.

Classlessness in Afrikaner society is reflected in almost every family's possessing the epitome of upper-class status and sometimes that of the middle class elsewhere – a servant. Income and the number of servants can be directly correlated among the Afrikaners with one important exception: at the lowest end of the Afrikaner income scale, such as among the railroad workers, there is a rise in the percentage of servants per family because having a servant becomes an absolute status necessity. To 'live like a Kaffir' is the ultimate in degradation. Throughout the poorer 'white' rural areas (where the population is still predominantly African or Coloured) there is a strong undertone of resentment among its supporters against the National Party for spending 'too much money' on African schooling and hospitals. Opposition United Party speakers – away from their relatively liberal colleagues in the cities – gain a local popularity by attacking the government for 'doing too much for the Kaffirs'. Although Dr. Verwoerd's assassin was mentally unbalanced, he was only one of thousands of poor whites and near whites who bitterly resented the increased sums expended on Bantu higher education and on the Bantustans schemes. Some Afrikaner farmers even sharply criticized Verwoerd's gift of 100,000 bags of grain to Lesotho.

Another influence towards 'classlessness' among Afrikaners is the relatively small number of Afrikaner surnames. There is scarcely an Afrikaans surname with strong upper-class connotations within Afrikanerdom. Afrikaners are also prone to extended family relationships with a multiplicity of cousin ties. Thus most Afrikaners recognize relatives throughout every walk of Afrikaner life.

In the early phase of nationalism, nearly all Afrikaners were in one class – uneducated if sober and industrious farmers – plus a sprinkling of educated *predikante* or ministers. This homogeneity was not peculiar to Afrikanerdom, but also indicative of the general poverty of all South Africa until the discovery of gold and diamonds. In the intermediate phase, wide class differences arose as some of the Afrikaners went into a new world. The gap between the educated and prosperous on one hand and the semi-educated and poor, such as the *bywoners* or landless farmers, on the other hand, reached its height in the 1930s. Afrikaner nationalism received an impetus from organized efforts to 'rescue' the 'poor white' Afrikaners. Today, middle- and lower-class Afrikaner groups have been able to gratify their wishes for higher levels of consumption. Egalitarianism marks Afrikanerdom once more, and the wide gap between the *armblanke* (poor whites) and the cultivated Afrikaner has been greatly lessened. Thus maturation of Afrikaner society has led to a further marked blurring of social boundaries as all classes of the society have become consumers at a fairly high level. Although social mobility is high, the paths from the bottom of Afrikaner society to the top have become well defined and there are few short cuts. It is no longer a unique distinction to become an Afrikaner pharmacist, admiral, bank president, or diplomat. The greater complexity of society and of increased international inter-dependence, especially in the business realm, has led to changing loyalties. An Afrikaner firm is at the apex of cigarette-selling in the world with notable successes in Great Britain, Europe, Canada, and Australia. The Afrikaner managerial team recognizes that its own loyalties have broadened and that it now looks back upon South Africa as a whole rather than upon Afrikanerdom alone.

The hypothesis that replacement of a bi-class by a tri-class social system precipitates crises in leadership does not apply with full force to Afrikaner or African nationalisms because of their unique interrelation-ship. Although Afrikaner nationalism has matured, it has never faced greater outside threats than it does today, producing a concomitant call for unity. Nevertheless, minor crises of leadership are developing in the once politically homogeneous Afrikaner *volk*. The first time a National Party caucus vote for a new Prime Minister failed of un-animity was in the 1958 choice of Dr. H. F. Verwoerd. But he domin-ated his party by the force of ideas to a greater extent than his party predecessors.

In viewing the Afrikaner and African middle classes, one is struck by the lack of a middle-ground meeting place for the creation of South African nationalism. Today, a truly unified middle class for the whole country would be composed of lower-class Afrikaner workers and upper-class Africans with unusual skills or in business. Instead of such groups providing the basis for the construction of a single national society, they are the very point of the most explosive contact.

Beneath the monolithic exterior of African society are greater tribal than class differences. The extended family system and the fact that nearly every African family has members or relatives both in the city and in the tribal reserves, also militates against the emergence of a true class system. In this kind of social structure the detribalized but ethnically identified African worker constitutes a modern 'tribe'. Even in the cities most minor altercations and even practically all the more significant mob fighting by Africans is still on a tribal basis. Yet it is only in the city that African nationalism finds a unity across tribal lines in its struggles. The heat of this lengthy struggle (the African National Congress itself dates from 1912) tends to melt new and tenuous class divisions.

Financially Africans are only beginning to gain significance. The traditional head (or hut) tax on all Africans is only starting to give way to a graduated income tax. It is unlikely that a majority of Africans liable to this tax actually pay it, but the figures are still revealing. In 1958, before the current boom, there were 1,025,749 income tax payers, of whom 920,743 were white. Among the 2,448 Africans, only three reported incomes of over the equivalent of $22,000. Once Africans reach the level of paying income tax, however, the distribution of taxpayers by categories of income is similar to that of the whites.

Under General Smuts's administration Africans of the upper strata, as defined largely by education and income, were exempted from various segregation laws such as the carrying of passes (but needed a document to prove it). Whether or not in time this tolerance would have produced an upper class of Africans 'loyal' to the whites is dubious. Some Afrikaners were themselves 'anglicized' by being drawn up into the English upper class in South Africa, but this move ironically intensified Afrikaner nationalism. Today the discrimination against Africans, from the college graduate in his business suit to the rural labourer in his overalls, is a strong force in overriding class consciousness among Africans. In African society the change from a bi-class to a tri-class system involves the replacement of traditional authorities by detribalized African leaders. Because the latter are unusually able and the former often inept, the old gives way to the new with fewer crises than may be expected. As with the Afrikaner, the need for unity and for the strongest leadership in the face of the ever-present 'enemy' makes the man who divides an unpopular one.

Although Africans in the Republic are quantitatively the most technologically advanced African group on the continent, occupational specialization is largely confined to the upper classes and has restricted the growth of nationalism in the lower classes. Thus the rural areas with their traditional tribal agriculture are relatively quiescent, with exceptions such as Pondoland and Sekukuniland. Also quiet are the gold mine compounds with their high percentage of 'foreign' labourers. Although some of the latter are specialized, they are kept from contact with nationalizing influences by the residential compound system. Moreover, a great number of them are foreigners from outside the Republic. But there is penetration of nationalism into the lower classes heightened by (1) their degree of urbanization and cultural Westernization, coupled with (2) the high visibility quotient every African carries with him, resulting in (3) the upper and middle classes being forced back into an identification with the lower class and thus broadening the social base of nationalism.

The staying power of tribal authority – even after two hundred years of contact with Western culture – was striking until weakened in recent years by government control and the manipulation of the chiefs and traditional authorities. This process of manipulation was also practised by the British with Seretse Khama in Bechuanaland and Sobhuza in Swaziland. Nevertheless, tribal authority declined. African nationalism has moved into the vacuum. The chief in the shadow of government power thus rarely emerges as an alternative pole of loyalty to the urban African population. In the enclave of Basutoland (now Lesotho) and in Swaziland, which adjoins South Africa, on the other hand, British toleration and encouragement of traditional authority have allowed it to become a conservative force resisting the growth of modern nationalism. There Swazi and Basuto loyalties have as yet to be transferred from the Swazi and Basuto peoples to their territories even though there are not, in these instances, competing tribes living within the same country.

The near-total exclusion of Africans from the Western political system and the workings of the 'pass laws' might drive Africans back to their traditional tribal political systems in the Republic were it not that the 'hated' government is attempting to encourage just that. The result is an extension of nationalism into the lower class to a greater extent than would otherwise occur. A wobbly government syllogism runs as follows: urban areas with African 'agitators' are politically disturbed; rural areas without 'agitators' are quiet; therefore, send the 'agitators' to the rural areas.

This final step was extensively carried out in the year following the Sharpeville shootings in March 1960. The result, however, was not the anticipated tranquillity in the countryside, but rather an extension of unrest and disorder to many rural areas. History may record that the base of African nationalism was thus broadened at a critical time with the assistance of Afrikaner nationalism.

In surveying the entire development of Afrikaner and African nationalism, we see clearly that class has been subordinated to a kind of group interest by almost all sections at almost all times. Now, as in the last century, being white counts for more than being skilled or rich. The labour movement (from 1900 to 1930) was predominantly English, Welsh, Cornish. The idea of the unity of the working class – white, black, brown – suffered its first defeat among English, Scots, Welsh, and especially Cornish workers in South Africa in 1913 and in the 1920s. When the Afrikaners trekked to the cities during the depression of the 1930s and grew in numbers until they formed the bulk of white workers, they merely extended the racial practices already followed. Old-time white labour leaders had hoped that the creation of an Afrikaans proletariat would lead to a Labour government, but the call of Afrikaner nationalism heavily sprinkled with racial fears made the non-Communist Afrikaner worker the close ally of the Afrikaner farmer and the new Afrikaner industrialist.

The Communist line in South Africa has been a wobbly one. Starting off with an appeal to all 'working men' it was twisted during the Stalinist purges of the 1930s towards the attainment of a 'Native Republic'. Thus a potentially flourishing organization was crippled because of Moscow's insistence that Afrikaner and English working men had to be told to fight for an African republic in which they would have a minor position because of their race. This 'line' was reversed less than a decade later, but by then many of the ablest comrades had been expelled and the sympathy of most white unions permanently alienated. What has survived is the Communist tactic of the 1930s that the party must be kept small, and that African nationalism must be encouraged through African organizations. There is thus a high degree of theoretical knowledge, discipline, and flexibility within a small party. But still the Communist Party places its greatest emphasis on nationalism and not upon class. Consequently all Africans, no matter how bourgeois, are considered in a common stream along with all whites who support the African cause.

On the non-Communist African side there has been little reason to consider class in the political struggle. Clements Kadalie's Industrial and Commercial Workers' Union of Africa, formed in 1919, has been the most successful African Union in South Africa. It set a pattern of fighting for African rights – economic and political – without reference to a class pattern involving whites. It resisted attempts by white Communists to control it at a time when this policy was also the party line. Subsequent African organizations have been formed on a racial basis (although not always with racist platforms) with an emphasis upon Africans of all classes. They have almost all continued to resist being turned to Communist ends by Communists of all races. Some have had only mixed success, such as the African National Congress; others have stayed well clear of Communist manipulation. Where the goal is the overthrow of the government as the Communists want, or even sweeping reforms as some African organizations seek, there will always be a measure of co-operation in a common cause. Until the recent change in the character of the multi-racial Liberal Party from a parliamentary party to one of all-out identification with democracy for all and hence with the African cause, there was no competition for the Communists in the 'freedom struggle'. The Liberal Party was born economically capitalist and staunchly opposed to totalitarianism of both the right and the left. Although some elements in it moved towards underground popular front alliances with Communists after 1962, and other elements embarked in a campaign of sabotage and bloodshed shortly after leaving the Liberals, the Liberal Party has not sought to introduce class issues as a means of either dividing or uniting the population. The relative weakness of the Liberal Party, both within the white electorate and among the African mass, is itself a symbol of how Afrikaner nationalism and

D

African nationalism have polarized political forces. In an alternate sense, they have also prolonged class concepts, and may be viewed as two huge feudal classes divided by colour. South African society thus lacks a true middle class and its integrating value for a South African nationalism. Class in its fullest sense has become synonymous with colour.

The possibility of including all classes within one nation through a broad economic advance derived from a high level of technology is characteristic of the Afrikaner case. Afrikaners have a national concern for the *armblanke* (poor whites). The intermediate phase of Afrikaner nationalism was given a strong impetus by the centenary celebration of the Great Trek of 1834–8. The enthusiasm engendered by the symbolic trek of thousands in 1938 was channelled into the *Reddingsdaadbond* (Relief Action Society) to uplift the poor whites (mostly Afrikaners and then equalling 45 per cent of the total Afrikaner population) and to make them strong components of the Afrikaner nation. Similar manifestations involved even far-flung offshoots of Afrikanerdom in Kenya, Argentina, and Angola. The *trek boers* of Angola were 'rescued' and rehabilitated with a sense of devotion. The so-called 'civilized labour policy' on the government railroads during the depression of the 1930s had displaced African pick and shovel workers with Afrikaner labourers at higher wages. Prime Minister Hertzog, backed by General Smuts, saw his primary responsibility as Prime Minister not to all the people of South Africa but to his people, the Afrikaners. The cry that 'our government' must help 'our people first' is still heard whenever a particularly costly Coloured school or African hospital is built. The wife of a current Cabinet Minister explained to the writer her opposition to the present expansion of Coloured education because 'our people need help first'.

Compared with the Afrikaners, there has not yet been an economic broadening of African society in the Republic, deriving from a high order of specialization, although it is far nearer to being one moderately prosperous society than other African societies to the north with the dichotomy of urban pay-cheques and rural subsistence. In 1960, of the 10,000,000 Africans, 895,312 had passed Standard V or primary school, 70,000 had passed the equivalent of junior high school, 14,421 had passed Standard X or high school. In January 1966 there were about

3,000 Africans who had graduated from a university. South Africa has outstripped other African countries in producing African university graduates from local institutions. However, the Republic has fallen far behind in the numbers of Africans receiving degrees abroad and will soon be behind several black African countries in producing graduates at home. The demand for secondary school education by Africans has been so tremendous as to force a dangerous expansion in relation to the number of trained teachers available. From 1949 to 1960, the number of secondary schools rose from 94 to 288, and to 309 in 1964. A marked increase of school matriculation passes, the rough equivalent of having completed grammar school G.C.E. 'O' level or high school, dropped from 47 per cent of the candidates in 1953 to only 17 per cent in 1960. Strong criticism was generated by Africans and also inside the government at this turn of events. However, according to government figures, the percentages of passes in 1965 had risen sharply to 61 per cent, and the total number of African matriculants was 827, or four times that of 1961.

That nationalist symbols and ideologies may be transmitted by a cosmopolitan group (such as white South Africans) before the social, political, and economic structures are articulated (as with the Africans) is clearly evident in South Africa. Day by day Africans can examine in minute detail the paraphernalia of nationalism laid out at full length by Afrikaners in public actions and in their press. It is simplicity itself to take a *stryddag* (struggle day – a party meeting) speech of the most emotional content and to substitute 'African' for 'Afrikaner'. Almost every charge the Afrikaners lay against the 'English' of one-time political control, domination of finance and commerce, of having exclusive private schools, is trebled by Africans when they want to charge Afrikaners. There are more than enough heroes to fill both pantheons. But whereas African society in the Republic has the quality of immediately available talent to give meaning to the less complicated political and economic structures of, say, Uganda or even the Congo, these actual structures in South Africa are in many ways more complicated than those of Western Europe. Unlike Ghana, with its cocoa monoculture and its gold- and diamond-mines, South Africa has a diversified fruit and grain export trade, giant steel mills, produces a tenth of its petrol or gasoline from coal, and has such complicated manufactures as the gold-mining machinery sold to Ghana.

Most whites in South Africa believe, correctly, that there are not enough educated and skilled Africans to take over all the administrative and technical posts in such a complex society at present levels of efficiency. Most whites miss the point that the development of African leadership in Africa has not meant that every non-African was immediately displaced. Furthermore, no country (including the U.S.A. and U.S.S.R.) has developed at a comparable stage without employing technicians from outside the national group. Current derogatory comments on African technical and administrative abilities are but new words to an old tune. In South Africa in 1910, when trucks were supplanting horse-drawn wagons, it was commonly asserted by whites that: 'The native will never be able to drive mechanical vehicles.' By contrast, senior government civil servants excuse various signs of inefficiency by pointing out that three million whites (in practice largely restricted to Afrikaners) 'must' furnish the administrative talent for a country of fifteen millions. There is a significant number of civil service posts where 'non-whites', limited though they are in training opportunities, would immediately improve the calibre of performance. However, despite what many leading Afrikaners feel are 'silly' job reservation laws, there has been a steady increase in the number of 'non-white' public servants in the Civil Service, education, and police. On the other hand, the Cape Town City Council has had notable success with Coloured traffic policemen, but the government has prohibited the hiring of more of them and legally barred the employment of 'non-white' parking-meter inspectors.

The principal efforts to give Africans necessary training are made, the white public is told by the government, with an eye to the growth of the 'self-governing Bantustans' (the Government prefers the expression 'Bantu Homelands'), in which such trained people may apply their talents over a wider area. The skills possessed in African society are thus often gained despite, as well as in some measure because of, the presence of an educationally advanced group which, to say the least, is ambivalent about passing on a wide range of skills or giving opportunities for this employment. None the less, Africans who show skills are employed to use them, and may reach labour-supervisory but not managerial levels in 'white' firms. In recent years the government has quietly employed growing numbers of Coloured and African workers, in the place of white workers, as postmen, telegram-deliverymen, and in many positions in the government-owned Railways, Iron and Steel Corporation, and similar organizations.

It is a common sight among the soaring skyscrapers and the honking traffic of Johannesburg to see a crowd of Africans wearing their tribal blankets *en route* to their first mine employment. Many who wait confused by a traffic light are from outside the Republic and have never driven in a motor-car. The contrast with a succession of poised urban Africans in smart single-breasted suits and carrying briefcases is a measure of the distance spanned in a few years. The interaction bet-ween Afrikaner and African, the daily cultural contact despite *apartheid* laws, especially in urban areas, enormously accelerates the rate of change among the undeveloped African group in the Republic.[1]

The transition from a rural, almost subsistence economy to a highly intricate money economy is one the Afrikaner has only recently com-pleted. The Africans are as yet only in midstream. Many deep South African problems are obscured by the still deeper racial issues. They include the transformation within a generation of the Afrikaner from a general farmer – and often a poor and even a landless one – to a pro-sperous exporting farmer or factory foreman or bank manager. A hundred years of industrial revolution in Europe are being compressed into one-half that period in South Africa. It is surprising that more non-racial disorders and dislocations have not taken place, and that South

---

[1] The extent of the concentration of African disposable income in urban areas, and in the white areas – both urban and rural – is not always recognized. The following figures are derived from research done by the South African Bureau of Market Research, and used by the Industrial Development Corporation in 1966. They are based on an assumed population growth and *per capita* income. Note that the disposable income of Africans in 'Bantu areas' was not expected to in-crease any faster than the income of Africans in 'Non-Bantu areas'.

Geographical Distribution of Estimated Disposable Income in Pounds
Sterling of the Bantu Population in 1963 and Projected for 1970

	1963	%	1970	%
Urban Areas	£226,723,000	60·3	£330,000,000	62·5
Non-African Rural Areas	£116,716,000	31·1	£153,750,000	22·1
Bantu Areas	£ 32,355,000	8·6	£ 44,050,000	8·4

Africa is among the nations of the world with the fewest strikes and industrial disturbances. While absence of strife in this area can have one explanation for African workers, it is also true of white workers and was so for twenty-five years before the present Afrikaner nationalist government came into power. Some of the strongest critics of the South African government concede that the legislation and operation of labour conciliation are among the best in the world.

The inherent complexity of the new economic techniques and the nature of modern ideologies have led to the necessity of mass recruitment into the new social, political, and occupational groups. The path has been a straightforward one for Afrikaners as they have moved from being a pastoral people with few occupations to a half-urban people in a complex economy with great occupational diversity.

There are three steps in this mass movement. The first is the movement from a simple rural society to a complex urban society. Secondly, comes the movement from African society (really societies) to Western society; and thirdly, the operation of the colour bar at almost all levels of society. The Afrikaner has been faced with only the first step. He has his church and other institutions to follow him to the city, and also his political power and racial advantage in seeking work. Nevertheless, Afrikaners have had an extremely difficult time in making this one transition. Great tears in the traditional fabric of Afrikaner *mores* are evident in the frequency of juvenile delinquency, prostitution, and loss of religious belief among those urban Afrikaners who change under the city's impact. In the lower class this disorganization shows in their 'sexsational' reading matter. Upper-class Afrikaner reactions are conveyed by numerous Afrikaans poems contrasting the pure rural life with the evil city life.

Many Afrikaners still think of their people as being essentially rural although the rural whites constituted only 46·8 per cent of the white population in 1911 (mostly Afrikaners) and only a minority of 14·0 per cent by the census of 1960. The influx of Afrikaners has been most marked on the Witwatersrand which had just over 50,000 whites in 1896 when industrialization began in South Africa and of these only some 6,000 were Afrikaners although it was part of the Transvaal. Today, the 377,000 English-speaking whites on the Rand are almost matched in numbers by the 338,000 Afrikaans-speakers.

Africans face all these problems several times over. Many studies reveal disintegration of African *mores* under pressures. Laura Longmore's *The Dispossessed*[1], a study of the sex-life of African women in Johannesburg, is one example. But before these society-destroying influences have run their course, Africans are confronted with forces emanating not only from the industrial revolution as outlined above, but also from the political forces of French, American, and Russian revolutions.

Skilled Africans have been most successful in breaking barriers into industrial occupations; racial barriers are higher in commerce. One result is a form of labour bootlegging. An African may be employed as a labourer or semi-skilled worker in a small shop, and actually perform skilled tasks for which he can usually demand under-the-table bonuses. In large factories jobs are reclassified from skilled to semi-skilled to allow the use of African workers. Afrikaners have shown no greater reluctance than other employers to use such tactics. In fact, they have taken the lead in shifting clothing factories to the borders of the African reserves where the ceiling on skilled African work does not apply.

That new industrial techniques lead to the necessity of mass recruitment into new occupations is as true for Africans in the Republic as it has been everywhere else. It means that eighteen years of Afrikaner nationalist government, with essentially conservative and traditional economic policies, have seen the greatest movement of Africans into urban and so-called European areas, and greater economic interdependence than ever before in South African history. This mobility is possibly not as great as the movement of Africans to the cities from 1940–7 under a war-time industrial boom. However, the stream was not reversed as the nationalists promised. Extraordinarily strict measures in 1960–2 kept down and slightly reduced the African population in Cape Town after a rapid burgeoning from 1948–60. In 1959 Dr. Verwoerd said that the final reversal of the African movement to the 'European areas' would not come until 1978. It is a sort of 'holy year' to some leading Cape Nationalists. While this estimate was more realistic sociologically than the naïve predictions of nationalists in 1948, it still needed to be modified in 1965 by Minister Daan Nel with

[1] London, Cape, 1959.

the flat statement that the reverse flow would not begin as planned, although sharply corrected by the Prime Minister in the secret parliamentary caucus. This partial shattering of the original economic theories and timetable of *apartheid*, backed by a host of laws and political exhortations, has come from the apparently inexorable pressure from industry for mass recruitment. Most of the social and political grievances of Africans are intensified when the occupational recruitment is not accompanied by recruitment into new social and political groups. Nationalist practice has accelerated the eventual breakdown of segregation by allowing more economic integration while assuming that only a man's hands may be recruited, omitting the rest of his person. It was not until 1959 – eleven years after *apartheid* started in earnest – that this fallacy was recognized and the Bantustan theory was seriously advanced in an effort to meet the problem.

As the years have gone by, the Nationalist government has paid greater attention to economic facts. Whereas nationalization of the gold-mines was a crude but popular idea when they came to power in 1948, it has disappeared. The Second Economic Development Programme, published early in 1966, gives more attention to African labour than ever before. The planners expect that whites will be proportionately less important in the total labour force. Between 1964 and 1970 the percentage of whites in manufacturing (27·6 per cent) and service industries (31·3 per cent) is expected to drop slightly despite immigration of skilled whites. The government posits a steady increase in living standards for all races on the economic boom continuing with the skilled manpower coming primarily from higher education among 'non-whites' and their advancement to higher positions.

To return to the political level, since about 1963, both Afrikaner and African nationalists have tried with success to break out of their original constituencies. The Afrikaner embrace of the like-minded English-speaking Europeans has paralleled the loosening of ties with both Britain and the Netherlands. The growth of this broader white support for the government has come at a time when the Afrikaner has largely emerged from what was generally accepted as an inferior class position *vis-à-vis* their English-speaking compatriots. Violent attacks by some Afrikaners on the notion of English ascendancy in a class breakdown were in themselves evidence of some feeling of inferiority. These have virtually disappeared.

It was not until the National Party had been in political power long enough not to gulp it down like a thirsty trekker in the Kalahari, and not until the Afrikaner businessman had developed some true economic strength that it was psychologically possible for the Afrikaner nationalist to open his arms to English support. The long tenure in office of the National Party also blunted the thoughts of many English businessmen that 'these upstarts' would soon disappear. It is the sense of permanence and consolidation about the revolutionary changes wrought by the nationalists which has finally led many English opponents of the National Party either to support it or to 'play ball' with it.

The composition of the Prime Minister's economic advisory group is proof of the fact that many staunch opponents of the nationalists have come to see that their support of South Africa as a country is more important. But, again, a decade ago neither Malan nor Strijdom would have been politically able within their own party to appoint 'liberal' economists and Jewish businessmen to official advice-giving positions.

An underlying suspicion of this opening to the English persists in the right wing of the National Party. Various financial manoeuvres involving Afrikaner and English business have been attacked as a 'sell-out' of Afrikaner principles. There are those Afrikaners who see in Harry Oppenheimer and his Anglo-American Corporation the devil incarnate. But financial deals between Oppenheimer and Afrikaner capitalists continue to be announced. The take-over of the very 'English' General Mining company by the very 'Afrikaans' Federale Mynbou was attacked by sections of the Afrikaans press.

A further indication of a changed climate in at least one respect lies in the number of judges of the Roman Catholic faith appointed by Prime Minister Vorster when he was Minister of Justice. Afrikaner–Catholic Church relationships are better today than at any time since the National Party came to power. This is not to say that Catholics have abandoned their criticism of *apartheid* or condone segregation inside their Church. Archbishop Hurley of Durban has been one of the strongest and most consistent liberal critics of the government. But only in the last few years has there been any strong Catholic support for government policy coupled with a sense of South Africanism. One of the strengths of the Catholic minority in South Africa is that its priests and bishops are 'home-grown' to a large extent and are really South Africans, be they also Afrikaner, English, or African. This is not nearly as true of the Anglican Church, which imports a large number of its priests and most of its bishops. The American Bishop in South West Africa and the former Archbishop Joost de Blank in Cape Town (English despite the name) are but two examples. Although it would be denied, it is not unfair to see in the elevation of Archbishop McCann of Cape Town to the red hat a sign that the Church of Rome is steering a mid-course between the liberalism expressed in Durban and the conservatism which emanated from Bloemfontein's Catholic Archbishop Whelan in recent years.

Afrikanerdom is broadening its attitudes in politics, business, and religion; in turn, it has become more acceptable to many of its political, business, and religious critics. Within the broadened white society of South Africa, it is likely that considerations of class will become more important unless they are again submerged by overriding considerations of survival of at least the 'white nation'.

The parallel African move from parochialism has been primarily in terms of movements outside of the Republic. Much of it involves relationships with foreign governments which we will consider in Chapter VIII. Suffice to point out here that African nationalism in the Republic was the deepest and most developed black nationalist movement in Africa. It displayed greater unity than the separate or collective Arab nationalisms. It had a broader constituency – based upon a higher level of modern public education – than Ghana or Nigeria where the roots went back farther. Thus the Africans in the Republic had little to learn from other African movements; they had nothing to gain in a material sense. Ideologically the position is not reversed; nationalism in African states is certainly equal in philosophy and sophistication to that of black South Africa. In the power realm, African nationalists in the Republic have lost a great deal of strength since the 1950s, whereas the African movements elsewhere have obviously come not only to national power but are now a major force in the United Nations. Although militarily and economically weak, the Organization of African States has a great deal to offer the South African movements – both internal and those in exile – if only in the form of some money with which to function.

African nationalism within the Republic has lost ground among whites as its appeal has shifted from one of peaceful co-operation and extension of rights to one of outright violence. In 1959, African National Congress President Albert Luthuli spoke in Cape Town's Drill Hall to an audience of about 1,500 people, most of them whites. While some of the whites were from the far left politically, the bulk of them whom the author interviewed on the spot were middle class and middle-of-the-road people. Most of them were members of the United Party and frankly curious to hear what Chief Luthuli would say. His speech appealed to them as he rang such familiar bells as peaceful co-operation, a democratic society, Christian brotherhood. Today one could not reassemble such a group nor could Luthuli legally address them, but there is reason to believe that the majority of those who found him 'reasonable' and a man to whom white South Africans must listen are today critical of Luthuli's statements and inclined to support the government in its charge that Luthuli is now only a dupe of the Communists.

If African nationalism has lost ground with the white mass as opposed to a handful of intense activists, it has gained some *rapport* with both the Asian and the Coloured communities. Many of the old antagonisms have broken down. Coloured prejudice against Africans has dropped markedly in the last decade. There is still resentment of the surplus of African males in Cape Town leading to sexual liaisons with Coloured girls. But the fact that Africans have taken over many Coloured jobs is less resented as the Coloured have in some cases moved to even better jobs. The influx of Africans into the Western Cape – beginning during the Second World War under Smuts but largely during the years of rule of the National Party, which pledged itself against such a development – has led to a better understanding of Coloureds and Africans as human beings. Some Coloured sports groups have been reluctant to abandon 'Coloured' teams for integrated 'Coloured and African' teams, and this has created some resentment. But overall, the increased education of both groups and their better economic position have contributed to better relations.

The educational gap between the Asian and white communities

in South Africa is also closing. This leads to some African criticisms because there is little change in the in-group feeling of the Asians and their reluctance to allow their daughters to be in contact with African males, even when the African males are better educated than the sheltered Asian girls. The deepest past resentment was the Indian economic exploitation of Africans. This has lessened as both groups have moved ahead economically. The frightful living conditions of the majority of both Asians and Africans in Durban two decades ago have been radically improved with the government's extensive housing programme. The stereotype held by so many Africans and English whites in Natal of the 'rich Indian' is no more true today, for life is a bitter struggle for the mass of Indians as it is for Africans. However, it has improved and there is no inclination to accept the standing government offers to Indians to be sent back to India.

The *rapprochement* between Afrikaner and English has a minor extension to Indians. One can certainly cite widespread Indian criticism of *apartheid* and resentment of many government measures. But the new Durban Indian university has been graduating its classes and never lacks for Indian entrants with adequate secondary school background. If Afrikaners have finally come to realize that the Indians are in South Africa to stay, so also have the Indians come to a *modus vivendi* of sorts with an Afrikaner government which to them appears to have come to stay for a long while.

Thus some of the lines dividing Coloured and Asian from Africans have been blurred in recent years and there is an overlap in the class structure, much of it stemming from a feeling that they are all collectively repressed by the government. At the same time and paradoxically, there is a greater acceptance of government planning by the two minorities and even an acceptance of the Afrikaner as a 'human being'. Fear of violence and anarchy is strong in both Coloured and Asian communities, and this militates against an even closer identification with Africans while it promotes a most noticeable drawing-in of the Coloureds and Indians towards the 'white *laager*'. It was not without forethought that at the close of a recent parliamentary session, Finance Minister Dönges spoke twice in a speech of a South Africa where five million hearts beat as one. When one does the addition of the white groups, one is left with the unmistakable point that he was including the Coloured and Indian groups. It was as though a new and broader society existed, one in which the differences were more of a class nature than a racial one. The idea did not last long, and the United Party helped to crush it by charging in Parliament that the Nationalists finally agreed with them; a true statement in many ways, but one calculated to make the Nationalists take back what Minister Dönges had said. Now that he is President Dönges, his embracing of the wider group takes on added significance.

CHAPTER V

COMMUNICATIONS IN THE TWO NATIONALISMS

The dependence of a growing nationalism upon mass communications is heightened in southern Africa because of its relative isolation from the rest of the world. Although white South Africans travel more miles *per capita* outside of their continent than any other people, including Americans, this was not true of Afrikaners in the days when their nationalism was developing, nor is it true of Africans today.

The mass-communications profile of South Africa differs from all other countries. It is by far the most important country not to have television. To its north television was pioneered by Rhodesia, Nigeria, Kenya, and Uganda, and has played a significant political role in Rhodesia especially. South Africa has the most comprehensive, well edited, and politically free press on the African continent. This may not be a great distinction compared with the greater press freedom in parts of Europe and North America. However, it is a fact that South African newspapers carry more and sharper criticism of the South African government than does the press of any other African country about its respective rulers. In common with many countries, radio is under government control. It is reasonably charged but denied by the authorities that the rapid extension of frequency modulation (F.M.) broadcasting in South Africa is a prelude to tight control of amplitude modulation (A.M.) and short-wave sets, particularly in the hands of non-Europeans. The inability of a T.V. or F.M. set to receive programmes from a great distance means that effective control of the air-waves is thus feasible in isolated South Africa.

The importance of radio in going over the borders of southern Africa was demonstrated in the Rhodesian crisis when the B.B.C.

rushed the erection of a radio transmitter in Butswana on Rhodesia's western border. South Africa itself has recognized somewhat belatedly that a part of modern diplomacy and war lies in wireless broadcasting, and has consequently opened an extra-territorial broadcasting station in Bloemfontein and a second one near Johannesburg to reach listeners in the African countries to the north.

Mass communications have accelerated the recruitment of both Afrikaners and Africans to their respective nationalisms. The first cultural movement among Afrikaners was built around the *Afrikaanse Patriot*, published near Cape Town in 1876. Afrikaner nationalism received a massive organizing boost with the establishment of the first large Afrikaans paper, *Die Burger*, in Cape Town in 1915. The new paper was hailed with deep emotion by Afrikaners as the corner-stone of their political thrust. Dr. Daniel François Malan left the ministry to become its first editor. Most of the early day-to-day management of the paper and most of the editorial writing was left to Advocate H. A. Fagan, later a cabinet minister (under General Hertzog) and the Chief Justice of South Africa's highest court, and to J. Steinmayer, who functioned as a managing editor. Dr. Malan put his primary energies into politics and resigned the editorship in 1924 to join Hertzog's Cabinet, and was the party leader when the Nationalists came to power in 1948 with himself as Prime Minister.

In the more heavily populated Transvaal, the party paper which battled through extremely difficult times was *Die Transvaler*, started in 1937. In its early days it was far more militant than *Die Burger*, and irritated United Party supporters immensely. *Die Transvaler's* opposition to South Africa's support of Great Britain in the Second World War made its building the focal point for a sharp and drawn-out riot. It is no coincidence that the first editor of *Die Transvaler*, Dr. H. F. Verwoerd, became party leader and Prime Minister after the undistinguished Strijdom period following ex-editor Malan. It has been overlooked by some writers that Strijdom was a sick man most of the time he was Prime Minister. A long-time supporter of his has described to the author how he led a group to see Strijdom in this period expecting to 'see the strong "lion of the north" when we were greeted by an emaciated tabby cat'.

The shift of Afrikaner political leadership from the Cape to the

Transvaal continues to have echoes in the politics of the newspaper world. For some years the voice of General Hertzog and later that of his lieutenant Klaas Havenga of the Afrikaner Party was found in the Johannesburg afternoon daily, *Die Vaderland*. In the 1950s and early 1960s, this paper was a tabloid, not as shrill a voice as *Die Transvaler*, and less effective politically, despite the advantage of a larger circulation. With the advent of A. M. van Schoor as editor, *Die Vaderland* moved to the political right of the *Transvaler* and began to represent that part of Transvaal Afrikanerdom which was suspicious of such seemingly liberal moves as taking in English supporters, and of 'doing too much' for the Bantu.

Over the last decade, the most influential and respected political writer in Transvaal Afrikanerdom has been Willem van Heerden, long-time editor of *Dagbreek en Sondagnuus*, a Sunday paper ostensibly 'rescued' from possible English control by Mr. Strijdom, but actually to block the move inside Afrikanerdom of the Cape *Nasionale Pers* to publish on the Rand. Although disagreeing with Dr. Verwoerd (then Chairman of the Board) on some issues, such as the treatment of the Coloured people, van Heerden was enormously successful in interpreting government policy to the Afrikaner mass and at the same time exerting restraint on the National Party when an extremist idea would threaten unity.

The division in the newspaper world parallel to that in the political world has kept *Die Burger* in Cape Town as pro-government; though through the pen of editor Piet Cillie, the paper spoke as a friendly critic of the government and was a moderate and thoughtful voice within the realm of European society. The polite accommodation between 'left' and 'right' in Afrikaans publishing (for each newspaper also had a book and magazine publishing aspect) was brought rudely to an end in 1965.

For many years Cape Town was the major city in South Africa without a Sunday newspaper. The most dynamic Sunday paper in the country was the *Sunday Times*, published in Johannesburg and sold in an ever-widening arc, reaching north to Salisbury and beyond, and south to the northern Cape. In 1963, a bright circulation man gambled in chartering a plane to rush the *Sunday Times* to the Cape in time for Sunday morning delivery, charged for it, and found it turned a profit.

Dagbreek followed, and this put it into competition with the large Saturday edition of *Die Burger*. The response from the controlling *Nasionale Pers* board was to launch their own Sunday paper, *Die Beeld*, and sell it not only in Cape Town but on the Witwatersrand as well. Despite a bitter intra-party struggle to prevent its entry into the Transvaal market, the paper met with early success.

Mass newspaper circulation has now spread to the whole Republic and is on the way to breaking down purely regional political differences among Afrikaners. The existence of two somewhat different political voices within Afrikanerdom is a function both of the unification of the country in technical matters and also of the huge majority the National Party has within Parliament and the practical fact that the effective opposition to many ideas comes not from the struggling United Party but from the ranks of Afrikaner Nationalism. More and more, Prime Minister Verwoerd, often privately critical of *Die Burger* and often indirectly criticized by it, found that the strongest support for some of his controversial policies (such as Bantustans) came from the Cape Town paper. *Die Burger*'s view is that Afrikaners have always been radical and that the kind of South Africa Afrikaners want can only be achieved by radical change. The basic thesis of this change is that only through recognition of the thrust of African nationalism (broken down into regional units under Bantustans) will there be a reasonable meeting of the demands of Africans and Coloured, and thus a viable future for Afrikanerdom. Admittedly, the *Burger* has been battling without much luck, although its ideas formed the basis of the 1966 Nationalist campaign. It is in the implementation of ideas that the *Burger* seems to have failed. With the establishment of *Die Beeld*, the traditionally radical approach is now in competition with the straight conservatism of much of the Transvaal Party.

There have been African-owned newspapers, but it is striking that the African press today is European-controlled even though African-edited, such as the daily *World* (formerly *Bantu World*). Although some papers are started throughout Africa by Africans, Republic Africans who have, on the whole, greater capital and more journalistic experience to start papers, do not do so on their own. The reason lies in part with the competition of the so-called 'English' newspapers, read by large numbers of urban Africans. In fact, Republic Africans lead the

E

sub-Sahara in literary and newspaper readership. The readership of some 'European' daily papers is as high as 25 per cent 'non-European'. The *Rand Daily Mail* is particularly liked by the African *élite*, especially since it replaced the expression 'native' with 'African'. The Johannesburg *Star* has the largest overall African readership. This newspaper integration is so potent for Africans who read English that it smothers efforts to establish a daily African press. A recent exception is the Johannesburg *World*, a 'penny' paper which shot ahead in circulation and influence in 1965–6. Educated Coloured people also regularly read publications aimed at Afrikaners. In recent years, *Die Burger* has published an increasing number of thoughtful and sometimes critical letters from Coloured people. But most Coloured readers prefer the more comprehensive and politically more acceptable English-language press.

It cannot be said that any one newspaper in the whole country has a significant influence on all groups, although the often sensational *Sunday Times* in Johannesburg is widely read by English, Afrikaners, and Africans throughout the Transvaal. Less than 10 per cent of the English read Afrikaans papers, and less than 35 per cent of Afrikaners read *die Engelse pers*. Perhaps 95 per cent of the upper classes of all groups and races read the English press as a first, second, or third paper.

Magazines mark another distinction between the previously rural Afrikaners and the Africans. The low cultural and moral tone of many best-selling Afrikans magazines has been evidence of this. In the last decade a better quality became apparent in *Die Huisgenoot*[1] (a *Saturday Evening Post*-type magazine), which has put *Die Brandwag* out of business, and in *Sjarme* (Charm). All African magazines are still tailored for detribalized Africans and are also cheaper than their potential competitors aimed at English readers. The *Ebony*- or *Life*-like picture magazine, *Bona*, has national circulation. Once-successful *Zonk* has folded, and the South African *Drum* has waned to where it is now a supplement to the African weekly *Post*. Foreign editions of *Drum* are sold throughout English-speaking Africa, while *Bona* has various vernacular editions. Sex, violence, African politics and African achievements are the main fare. The number of advertisements is

---

[1] Much earlier *Die Huisgenoot* had been a publication of literary merit, so much so that Mrs. Verwoerd wrote her M.A. thesis on its influence on Afrikaans.

higher than in many British publications and they are read with greater intensity.

State-controlled Radio South Africa provides four programmes – English, Afrikaans, a commercial channel in both these languages, and a Bantu programme. In addition, regional programmes are specially tailored, including some in Natal in Indian languages. The Bantu service covering numerous languages is backed by a large – the largest of all the services – and well-trained African technical and editorial staff. Radio South Africa's English and Afrikaans radio programmes are commonly listened to by Africans and preferred by the educated Africans. The shift from A.M. to F.M., calculated to control reception of foreign broadcasts, is far from completed. At present the thousands of Africans who own radios capable of short-wave reception are free to listen as they please to London, Peking, or Moscow. The time may come when short-wave and A.M. sets will be banned to control dissemination of new and hostile propaganda from abroad, although this possibility is strongly discounted by knowledgeable Afrikaans journalists.

The absence of television stems partly from a drive to shield Africans, but more importantly from the presence of the old Afrikaans–English split. It would be inordinately expensive to produce the same quality Afrikaans programmes as English programmes, which could be purchased abroad. Hence the struggle over European languages and not finance keeps South Africa behind such poorer African countries in the use of television. Often overlooked is the impact which television would have on advertising budgets. Experience in other countries suggests that the lowest-circulation papers suffer most, and it is the Afrikaans papers which find it most difficult to compete for advertising revenue with the English press. They would suffer and the political voice of the National Party would be muted, for despite a noticeable slipping in the traditional impartiality of Radio South Africa, it cannot have as high a content of pro-National Party propaganda as do some Afrikaans papers. Another factor is that the rural influence in the National Party would demand television for itself at a high cost in such a vast country. In the 1966 election, a Nationalist reply to a United Party taunt was: 'Yes, Rhodesia has television, but they would rather have a S.A.S.O.L. (gasoline from coal plant)!'

Motion pictures or cinemas and the theatre are ideally adapted to the aims of Afrikaner nationalism because the audiences can be restricted and the 'black' man kept from looking over the 'white' man's shoulder. Films for Africans are censored differently from those for whites. There is virtually no restriction on plays. Imported books are occasionally banned. But more often the expensive hard-cover edition is allowed in, while the cheaper paperback with a sensational cover, the one more likely to be purchased by Africans and young people, is kept out.

The African population of the Republic receives in ample measure the force of Western culture. Political ideas from abroad are not really blocked because of the wide readership of the English-language press. Paradoxically, there is no country in Africa where more forceful personal attacks can be made on government officials without reprisals than in South Africa. Although the English press does screen out some economic news favourable to Communist countries, for many years *New Age*, the Communist-edited newspaper with the greatest circulation in Africa, was published in the Republic. In addition to the ideas transmitted through the conventional communications media, nowhere in the world can a higher percentage of 'underdeveloped people' see so easily, many of them every day of their lives, the benefits available to more fortunate men. Furthermore, because some cream spills over to the poor relation, there is a distinct taste for a better material life. Africans in South Africa have four times as many cars (100,000) *per capita* as do the citizens of the Soviet Union (575,000). In some smart downtown Johannesburg clothing stores, half of the higher-priced men's suits are sold to Africans. In the tribal reserves, where there are fewer European 'models' to advertise what a high standard of living can mean, local-boys-made-good return from the city as walking advertisements. Expectations of economic advance are high throughout both urban and rural African society.

In spite of the open nature of the communications media and the daily interrelation of white and African society in the streets and in offices, the door is virtually closed to cultural and political contact of one group with another across colour lines. The three white representatives of the Africans who sat in Parliament until removed in 1959 were important not for their tiny voting strength, but as voices of some

African opinion. Their replacement by tribal political structures has not been accepted by a majority of urban Bantu, and the clumsy arrangements for chiefs to have 'ambassadors' in urban areas are inadequate as an outlet for politically conscious Africans.

Despite what has been said about the freedom of criticism in the South African press, there are varieties of censorship by the government beyond those normal in the United States or United Kingdom. Regulations on prison stories are very strict and constitute a major complaint that the English press has against the government. On the one hand, the government has been extremely annoyed in the past when the press has exposed various inequities in the use of prison labour on farms and mistreatment of prisoners. On the other hand, sensational journalism has resulted in some flagrantly untrue charges against police and prison officials. Some of these stories have gone round a world thirsting for news of evil-doing in South Africa, whereas the subsequent repudiation of many of the allegations and the 'clearing' of charges by such reputable bodies as the International Red Cross have not been printed by newspapers carrying the original charges.

But at a deeper level there is absolute prohibition on the importation, printing, or dissemination of what the government defines as Communist propaganda and publications of African nationalist movements. Much of the controlling legislation is of recent origin: a decade ago Marx's Communist Manifesto could be printed – and was – in South Africa without penalty. Today, the Communist-front papers such as *New Age* followed and preceded by other party papers different only in name, are suppressed. As late as 1958, *New Age* was probably read by more Africans than any other political publication in South Africa. In remote African reserves, one would be asked questions about alleged American germ warfare in Korea, the great successes of the Soviet Union and all the current ideological catch phrases. Readership of *New Age* probably exceeded 200,000 for each weekly issue, as copies were passed from hand to hand. Its liberal competitor, *Contact*, never approached its influence, and has now dwindled away from lack of funds as well as the rapid turnover of staff as one man after another has been prohibited from association with it.

In the broad realm of communication it is easy to overlook the vital importance of private communication in the transmission of ideological inspiration. The free-and-easy atmosphere of the late 1940s in Johannesburg, Cape Town, and Durban, with many racially mixed parties within a particular ideological set, close association in and out of the Soviet mission as a wartime ally, and speechmaking at political and labour meetings, all provided the dissemination of both non-Communist liberal and Communist ideas.

The successively stringent restrictions on such communication through the 1950s and continuing even more strictly into the 1960s closed one avenue after another. The effect of bannings on writing and speaking, the number of people under house arrest or in preventive detention, drastically cut down on the spread of ideas and, in some ways more importantly, on the inspiration to protest which many whites (the principal targets of government legislation and police action) conveyed to the non-white groups. Above and beyond this the legal and extra-legal coercion involved in the various government moves severely cut down on recruitment to both the Communist and to the separate liberal groupings. The Communists were better organized and had better discipline, but the various successful government trials have shown that relatively few new people from either the white or non-white communities were recruited after the atmosphere changed. The relative ease with which the government infiltrated left-wing movements with such secret agents as Officer Ludi was a reflection in part of the paucity of recruits and pressure within the left to accept almost anyone at face value.

One of the few avenues for the non-written transmission of ideas which remained open into the 1960s was the National Union of South African Students. Although virtually barred from Afrikaans-speaking campuses, N.U.S.A.S. remained the dominant voice on English-speaking campuses. Although under severe attacks from government spokesmen and not always popular with the authorities at its own universities, N.U.S.A.S. was long the most active disseminator of liberal thought. A reaction against N.U.S.A.S. took place when it was discovered that some of the leadership had ideas considerably to the left of the majority of the student members and, in fact, some N.U.S.A.S. leaders were convicted of sabotage. The movement was given a 'shot in the arm' by the much-publicized visit of Senator

Robert Kennedy in 1966, which stirred young university people on 'English' campuses and was not without a significant impact even at Stellenbosch University. Nevertheless, the gradual success of the government in establishing the new university colleges has had the effect of removing most African, Coloured, and Indian students from daily association with liberal-minded whites. In the future, those non-whites who are given permission to attend the 'open' universities will be primarily in such fields as engineering and science where the political motivations of students tend to be submerged in their studies.

Underground publications have not been successful in South Africa as they were in parts of German-occupied Europe. There have been a few mimeographed efforts to keep the spark of revolution burning at least feebly, but the risks of being caught and the difficulty of distribution have been too great. There is such a demand by foreign intelligence and scholars for ephemeral underground material that it is more practical to publish illegally with the idea of selling copies abroad to raise funds than as a means of reaching the masses.

An extremely limited circulation has been achieved in South Africa by *Assegai*, which began publication in mimeographed form in January 1963, and soon shifted to forty printed pages in a smaller format to fit ordinary envelopes. The cover of the first issue featured the slogan of Mao Tse Tung, 'A single spark can cause a prairie fire,' as well as the continuing use of the hoary slogan, 'Workers of the world unite, you have nothing to lose but your chains.' A mild effort at deception has been to print occasional extra concealing covers, such as 'Oliver Twist by Charles Dickens', but the police were soon on to this.

Within the Republic a technique most exploited in 1961-3 was the painting of slogans in prominent places. 'Down with tyrants', 'Vorster is a Nazi', and simple 'Freedom', had many variations. Most of them were done with swiftness and stealth in the dead of night by Europeans using airbrushes and sprayguns. For a while the authorities were slow to even cover them up and hampered by the small fines for defacing property. Stiff legislation and roving police-cars have almost eliminated the sign-painting. Throughout 1965, only a handful of signs were painted, such as 'Free Mandela', and almost all of them in Johannesburg. Activity dwindled because some of the sign-painters were arrested and convicted on other charges, while others felt that the chance of being caught and the price to be paid were not worth the possible gain. Indeed, in the years following Sharpeville, when for a long time the press reported many isolated cases of sabotage (and many others were unreported), the only visible evidence to the average white or black citizen in the main urban centres that South Africa was not proceeding on a tranquil path, were the signs.

There is considerable doubt as to the value of the sign-painting to the cause of the African nationalists. A Johannesburg stockbroker, being driven to work into the city centre from his luxurious home in the northern suburbs, was certainly jarred by seeing a huge red slogan on the side of a modernistic overpass, 'Down with Verwoerd'. It effectively reminded him that beneath all the hustle and bustle of the great financial city of Johannesburg, black and white men were quietly plotting to overthrow the society. It may have pricked his conscience and led to greater concern for the welfare of his servants or, to quote the words of one businessman: 'I think the signs convinced me that I must support the Institute of Race Relations[1] in its work for better understanding and changes in the laws.' But among many of those driving to work, including many who favour amelioration of many *apartheid* laws and whose personal relationships with Africans could scarcely be faulted, the signs were a reminder that the Afrikaner politicians and police officials who inveighed against the enemy within were not making their case out of hot air. In the jargon of economics, it is the author's view that the whole sign-writing campaign was counter-productive. In one night, two men in a fast-moving automobile can paint an image for a city of one million that there are many thousands plotting revolution when, in fact, the Malabas (Jones) of Soweto are more interested on their way to work in reading the same *Rand Daily Mail* to see whether the Orlando Pirates won their big soccer match.

Publications backing African nationalism in the Republic are published abroad, but they are banned for importation and have a miniscule *sub rosa* circulation. Among the more important are the *African Communist*, a monthly newspaper produced in London by the South African Communist Party in exile, which does serve as an ideological debating ground for the party *élite*. The liberally oriented *New African* ('The Radical Review') began publication in Cape Town but shifted

[1] That is, the South African Institute of Race Relations.

to London under pressure. The Pan African Congress has been intermittent in its publications. While Patrick Duncan was representing it
in Algiers, he produced a regular mimeographed magazine in French
and focused on South Africa. More recently, the African National
Congress's weekly mimeographed effort, *Spotlight on Africa*, produced
in Dar-es-Salaam, has carried the A.N.C. message. All of these publications are now primarily directed at an audience outside of the Republic.
None of them has even a minor readership in South Africa, although
individual copies do enter the Republic.

There is no doubt that the South African government has succeeded
in suppressing the mass communications of the African nationalists
within the country. No effective way around this (such as spreading
of news mouth-to-mouth) has been found. In the past, African nationalists could rely heavily upon parts of the English press to put some of
their message across. In the process of covering a news story of a
potential general strike, in, say, Johannesburg, the newspapers would
print statements by the strike organizers. At times this was their
principal way of reaching their many and far-flung supporters. Today,
the English press is not only legally barred from printing statements
from a long list of banned people, but editors appear personally cautious
about blowing up the statements of a few individuals to help them create
a mass following.

African nationalism in its revolutionary garb is presently unable to
gradually build up a mass organization with mass communications.
However, in a crisis situation, the outside organizations might well
communicate with the mass of the African people on a one-shot basis.
Various 'freedom radios' have been on the air in South Africa. With the
use of sophisticated and expensive electronic gear purchased in the
United States, authorities are usually able to eliminate an underground
station given enough time; it is more difficult to move against one sud-
denly on the air from just beyond South Africa's borders.

In sum, one can conclude that the role of mass communications for
both Afrikaner and African nationalisms has changed markedly. For
the former, the role is less that of spreading the party gospel than extending a dialogue within the party and between the party and the non-
Afrikaner nationalist whites. For African nationalism, the relatively
easy access to millions of urban Africans is now ended. The building

up of an African personality by the English press is less likely. Thus the chances of creating a country-wide movement held together by the charisma of one or two men are slim indeed.

The tendency seems to be for many individual Africans to assume a local leadership role in primarily local matters. There is no doubt that Prime Minister Matanzima of the Transkei is the best-known of all African leaders in the Republic who are outside jail or restrictions. The chiefs tend to benefit from the present state of affairs. So also do previously unimportant bodies of Africans such as school boards and advisory town councils. In Soweto (the south-western townships of Johannesburg and one of the great African cities of the continent), a place on the key council is growing in importance. Issues tend to focus on improving a specific local grievance, such as bus service, police patrols to protect honest people against criminal gangs, or the operation of beer halls and cocktail lounges. This the government encourages with great caution lest these municipal matters be funnels for national issues. They are recognized along with tribal councils as training-grounds for political advance. Thus some Afrikaners favour them as healthy steps towards the African management of the African side of separate development while, conversely, some Africans see them as opportunities to create pressure groups either to modify or to directly attack government policies.

What are lacking in new locally based councils aiming for wider political roles are communications suitable for mass recruitment. It is unlikely that the government will allow channels to be opened up.

CHAPTER VI

AFRIKANER NATIONALISM –
TO THE FINAL STAGE

EARLY STAGE

Afrikaner nationalism has had a long and successful trek since it emerged from the ashes of its burned-out farmhouses after the Boer War, or, as Afrikaners call it, 'The Second War of Independence'. In the minds of Afrikaners, the sense of moving towards a destiny and from a past has roots in the Great Trek of 1836 away from British rule and in the protests of such libertarians as Adam Tas condemning the iniquities of a Dutch colonial governor in the early eighteenth century.

Today, if one drives across the Adam Tas bridge into the lovely village of Stellenbosch, with its numerous churches, university buildings, and Cape Dutch houses, into the *braak* or village square with whitewashed and thatched-roof buildings, or sits on the *stoep* of Adam Tas' homestead and looks across the vineyards up to the rugged peaks of the Hottentot Holland Mountains, one feels that perhaps South Africa has changed less than the world. Outwardly, there are minor changes. The Coloured community is less scattered residentially and more of them are successfully self-employed. The Bantu have been added, but they must sleep at night in a location on the edge of town. And yet, even in this citadel of Afrikaner traditionalism, if one looks inside the minds of men, it is a new world and a new Afrikanerdom.

An early characteristic of nationalism is the restriction of the sentiment of nationalism largely to the upper class; this phase was largely passed through at the turn of the twentieth century with the *taal* or language movements at the Cape and the 'Boer War' fought by the Transvaal and Orange Free State. And yet the restricted focus of Afrikaner nationalism was shown in Dr. D. F. Malan's appeal in the

Afrikaans intellectual centre of Stellenbosch in 1921 for the use of Afrikaans. His plea was of necessity still made in High Dutch! The young Jan Smuts, as a student in the 1890s, wrote to his betrothed in alien English because High Dutch was too stiff and Afrikaans then too much of a 'kitchen language'.

A second early characteristic is respect for the rule of law, as set down by the nationalists, which increases as nationalism advances. At this final stage of nationalism, respect for the rule of law is now high among all Afrikaners. This is reflected in the absence of lynchings and also (in a perverse sense) in the steady stream of convictions of Afrikaners for breaking the laws against miscegenation. The fact that Afrikaner policemen are not infrequently 'brought to book' for using strong-arm tactics on Africans and convicted by Afrikaner judges indicates that the society stands by the law even while individuals break it. (The issues of '90-day detention' and '180-day banning' and 'house arrests' revolve around civil rights legislation, and not the carrying out of legally valid laws.)

Much of the world had difficulty during the Rhodesian crisis in understanding the reluctance of South Africa to go to the assistance of the white government of Ian Smith. But a major factor in the judgement of the South African government, resting quite sturdily on the individual consciences of Afrikaner supporters, was the illegality, as they first saw it, of the Unilateral Declaration of Independence, along with their adherence to a principle of non-interference in the affairs of another country.

Afrikaner nationalism's violent phase was the 1899–1902 Boer War or the Second War for Independence (following the earlier Transvaal War, in which the British were beaten). Approximately 20,000 to 26,000 Boer women and children out of a small population died in British 'concentration camps'[1] – largely from neglect, malnutrition, poor medical services and sanitation, rooted in British maladministration. Memories of this have been an embittering acid in the Afrikaner soul. Later nationalism inflamed anti-British feeling on this score to greater heights than that felt by most of the Boers who actually fought

[1] To try to establish a precise figure agreed upon by all South Africans is to start a new war. What is germane is that feelings continue to run high over the figures used.

and whose wives and children died in the camps. But today this feeling is subsiding rapidly.

A third characteristic is the importance of a charismatic leader in the early phases of nationalism. Within Afrikanerdom, the leaders from Kruger to Hertzog to Malan to Strijdom declined in their charisma as party organizations became stronger. In the Boer War, a handful of generals exercised far greater appeal than has any South African military man since.

As Prime Minister, Verwoerd stood head and shoulders above his cabinet in his strong personality. He exercised a charismatic hold primarily on the less-educated sections of the Afrikaans middle and lower classes and was also tremendously effective with his officials and top Afrikaner politicians. The author will never forget waiting to see him outside his Cape Town office one time when an informal Cabinet meeting was going on inside. As the meeting broke (after – one learned later – considerable strong criticism from the Prime Minister), the Cabinet shuffled out the door as though they were chastised bad boys. It is a curious fact about Afrikaner politics under Dr. Verwoerd that while he turned on the charm with great sincerity and skill, he did not depend upon it to carry many unpopular ideas. He was forever analysing the trend of politics and trying to sell ideas to his own group on facts rather than trying to gain their support by his charismatic appeal alone. It was often said by observers within the National Party that Prime Minister Verwoerd should have taken a stronger and more positive lead – to develop Bantustans faster, for example – and not have been so sensitive to the rumblings from the right wing. Verwoerd underestimated his own political power in proceeding with great caution towards goals he repeatedly said were vital. Perhaps he had in mind the fact that Afrikaner Nationalist leaders are always replaced from what appears to be the political right, never from the left inside the party.

There were many opportunities to make a cult of leadership out of Verwoerd. His truly miraculous escape from two bullets fired at point-blank range through his head did lead some Afrikaners to speak of his survival as divine will. But he had not personally exploited this kind of appeal, with the exception of a solitary reference to the hand of God.

Prime Minister John Vorster has followed the pattern – which

Verwoerd may have intended to break if able to name his successor – of the new Prime Minister emerging to the political right of the Cabinet and caucus. In the early months of Vorster's leadership, the world press was so preoccupied with references to his activities in the Second World War, and to his role as Justice Minister with control of the Police, that his personality as a Prime Minister was obscured. Although referred to as a 'strong man' as a Cabinet Minister, he had not developed many of the strengths Verwoerd possessed, such as an image of avuncular cordiality, patience, and shrewdness on the international scene, strong appeal to English-speaking whites and respect, if not in some cases a genuine affection, from some Africans. However, at the time he took the reins, Verwoerd had not displayed these characteristics.

On balance, one can say that Afrikaner nationalism, even under Verwoerd, did not depend upon charismatic leadership nearly as much as on a hard-working and tightly organized party machine, down to and up from the constituency level. The numerous upsets of sitting M.P.s in the Nationalist constituency nominations in late 1965 showed a vigorous grass-roots politics and an absence of *diktat*.

A fourth characteristic of early nationalism is the development of an ideology with a wide appeal to many seemingly diverse groups. Afrikaner nationalism went through this stage in the past when broad ideological alliances were formed. The notable example was the Pact Government (1924–33) between Afrikaner leader Hertzog and the Labour Party. The latter was, by South African standards, relatively liberal, and many of its leaders had close ties with and sympathies for African workers. The anti-English-speaking leaders of Afrikaner nationalism and the Labour Party made strange bedfellows.

How then does one explain the reaching out of Afrikanerdom in the 1960s to a wider constituency if it has become a matured nationalism? To some extent, the adherence to Afrikanerdom of English-speaking South Africans has been on the ideological terms of Afrikanerdom. The need to broaden the base of support when faced with what many Afrikaners believe will be attack from abroad is also a factor. But within a theoretical approach which sees nationalism as broad at the beginning and narrowing down as it reaches its objective, the broadening of Afrikanerdom is not a function of Afrikaner nationalism as much as it is the earliest stage of a broad South African nationalism which today is extended with slight warmth to the English and in a tepid way to the Coloured community or *bruin* (brown) Afrikaners.

Fifth among early indications of nationalism is when significant masses are left untouched. This period in Afrikaner nationalism was relatively short. Although separated from the Boer states, there was Afrikaner activity in Cape Town under the British Crown from the 1870s onward, including the formation of the Bond under J. H. Hofmeyr, Sr. There are different ways of interpreting just where the deepest Afrikaner stream ran through the 1930s and 1940s. To some the small rump party of Dr. Malan's purified nationalists, represented only by Strijdom in the Transvaal, was still a minority party without mass Afrikaner support. However, a more reasonable interpretation is that while Malan was certainly at the heart of the nationalist drive, Hertzog, Havenga, and others were by no means outside it, not to exclude such Hertzogites as Fagan, who later supported Smuts. In the 1920s and 1930s, the cry of Afrikaners for a broad range of rights had become the voice of the Afrikaner masses, regardless of political party.

A sixth characteristic of the early period is the strong drive for upward mobility among the middle sectors. This is one aspect of Afrikaner nationalism which has had a curious persistence and has given rise to some social tensions about 'snob' schools. Two generations ago the drive for upward mobility is what created anglicized Afrikaners, many of whom were absorbed by the ruling British classes. Thus there are Van Zyls who never read an Afrikaans newspaper, although the language is taught in the schools. The strongest (in intensity, but not in numbers) political opposition to Afrikaner nationalism has come from this group of Afrikaans descent. Because of this early social absorption and in an effort to catch Afrikaner votes, the predominantly English-speaking United Party puts up about half of its candidates from among persons with Afrikaans names, although a number of such candidates send their children to 'exclusive English schools', as the Nationalists call them in derision.

The seventh characteristic is a great dependence on foreign example. The two powerful nationalisms in South Africa have both been deeply affected by those historical periods during which they, in a common but distinct process of moving towards nationalism, entered a mimetic stage: most Afrikaners first looked abroad for a model in the 1930s just as most Africans are taking their first real look abroad today. Thus Afrikaner nationalism just before its final rise to power in 1948 was affected by the nationalistic ideologies of Europe before the Second World War. Whatever was anti-British looked attractive to Afrikaners. To many, Hitler and National Socialism were preferable to Chamberlain and democracy. According to a court decision on a libel action, Dr. H. F. Verwoerd, then editor of the party newspaper in the north, *Die Transvaler*, supported Nazi Germany. But it must also be said that Verwoerd opposed the *Ossewa Brandwag* (O.B., a militantly anti-British group) so strenuously that a group of angry O.B.s surprised him in his driveway one night and threatened to assault him. Various Nazi imitations sprang into existence, such as Oswald Pirow's New Order and the anti-Semitic 'Grey Shirts'. The *Ossewa Brandwag* ('Ox Wagon Sentinel') was more indigenously Afrikaans and gained significant strength throughout South Africa. In time it challenged the *Nasionale Party* as the torch bearer of Afrikaner nationalism.

All these movements had a superficial quality, their vitality vitiated by distance from the source in Europe and the traditional antipathy to Britain. The National Party, led by Dr. D. F. Malan, clashed with the O.B. during the Second World War over Nazi associations. A bitter struggle ensued until the O.B. was smashed in 1944. Because much of the British propaganda against Germans in the First World War had later been exposed as false, Afrikaners were very slow to realize the actuality of the mass murders of Jews in the Second World War. As the facts became evident and the issues clarified, most Afrikaners saw the Second World War in a different light and the Afrikaner contribution to the war against the German Reich was strengthened. It was significant that the Moderator of the Cape Dutch Reformed Church, Rev. J. S. Gericke, in his spirited oration at Verwoerd's funeral, made his theme the comparison of the Afrikaner *volk* with Israelis in wanting to live in peace but being subject to 'vicious attacks'.

A few individuals who privately believed in National Socialism are still active as members of the National Party but are far outnumbered by those who see it conflicting with traditional Afrikaner values, and who accordingly oppose it. Newspaper editorials in the 'English' press of South Africa and in Britain in the 1940s anticipated a full-fledged Nazi government in South Africa by 1960. Professor Keppel-Jones, formerly of Natal University and later of Queens in Canada, is one of many who continued to attack the Nazi 'image' after it had ceased to be the model. Keppel-Jones predicted in his 1948 history of the future, *When Smuts Goes*, that the great *pogrom* would take place in 1956. In fact, that was the year a Jewish group presented Dr. Malan with a silver plate as the 'Moses of the Afrikaner people'. Subsequently Nationalist politicians inaugurated a number of synagogues, including the Great Synagogue in Johannesburg, opened by Finance Minister Eben Dönges, one of those associated with anti-Semitism in the 1930s. The Afrikaner government has given extraordinary aid to Israel in critical times, and Dr. Malan was the first Head of State to visit the new Israel. Today, English clubs have more anti-Semitic barriers than do Afrikaans clubs.

In extremis, Afrikaner nationalism may still come to imitate the Fascist dictatorships of Europe, but for at least nineteen years these models have been thoroughly discredited among the majority of Afrikaner leaders. Despite war-time charges to the contrary, both Malan and Strijdom were anti-Nazi in belief, although staunch segregationists. Details of Malan's successful undercover fight against Nazism inside Afrikaner nationalism have recently come to light. Nevertheless, the influence of former Nazi supporters in the nationalist caucus has led to strenuous attacks by the white opposition against their presence in the government.

The 'Nazi' image which first the United Party, later the *Rand Daily Mail* and much of the world press tried to place on the late Dr. Verwoerd failed in the end. Remarkably, Verwoerd was complimented in death by many who continued to disagree with his politics for being an effective leader of his country. Notable in their praise were United Party leader Sir de Villiers Graaff, the *Rand Daily Mail* and Johannesburg *Sunday Times*, the *African World* in Johannesburg, and South African Jewish periodicals.

Prime Minister Vorster began his office with a greater handicap than Verwoerd, and certainly with more doubters in his own party. Even his rival, Minister Ben Schoeman, who did not finally contest Vorster, had opposed Vorster's candidacy on the National Party ticket in 1948 because of war-time differences.

The end of the mimetic stage of Afrikaner nationalism was pointed

F

up in 1962 when opponents of the new so-called 'anti-sabotage' law compared it to laws in Ghana, Hitler Germany, Spain, the Soviet Union, and Portugal. Certainly the oversimplified 'Nazi' label that is often stuck on the Nationalist Party is an anachronistic epithet. The law – wise and necessary or vicious and oppressive – is not borrowed from abroad but is South African. The mimetic phase of Afrikaner nationalism is largely closed.

Accompanying the period of dependence on foreign example, one usually finds an exaggerated feeling of anti-imperialism. Afrikaners may have reached the height of exaggeration during the Second World War under the stimulus of Radio *Zeesen*, whose virulently anti-Allied broadcasts were widely listened to in South Africa. One in no way excuses the poor British management of its concentration camps in the Boer War when one discounts many of the stories used to whip up anti-imperialist feelings as late as 1955. No doubt there was ground glass found in some of the food in a camp, but almost two generations later the number of people whose grandmothers had died from such a dastardly British trick had multiplied out of all credulity. Since the coming of the Republic, this phase of exaggeration for which many verses in many chapters could be cited, has ended. Afrikaners were the bitterest anti-imperialists as long as Great Britain or her settler sons controlled their destinies, but Afrikaners are now the political power with their own 'empire' and such feeling has declined. Afrikaner resentment lingers in the financial and business worlds, which is still four-fifths 'English-'controlled.

Despite the freshness of their own struggle, few Afrikaners recognize that those deep human emotions – the desire for self-determination and for equality of treatment, and the pride which burned deep into the Afrikaner soul and sparked the anti-colonial fight – are the same fundamental emotions producing similar determination in African hearts. It was not until the 1966 election campaign that Verwoerd and others drove this point home in support of their Bantustan policy against criticism of the United Party and the Afrikaner Republican far right. But on this issue world sympathy has clearly shifted from the Boers to the Africans.

INTERMEDIATE STAGE

In Afrikaner nationalism, the intermediate stage has been virtually completed in all its aspects. Loyalty values have shifted to the middle and lower groups, although what was the Afrikaner lower class was always truncated by the Africans below it and is now lessened in prosperity. In 1949, in a great outpouring of Afrikaner emotionalism, the *Voortrekker* Monument had been dedicated in memory of the Great Trek over a century before. Nationalistic slogans were widespread in the schools by 1950. Compulsory legislation required all Afrikaans-speaking children to attend schools in that language and the curriculum in most parts of the country is to a degree adapted to 'Christian National Education', as opposed to British liberal education. In 1961, the Administrator (or governor) of the Transvaal called upon all white schools to inculcate the importance of defending white, Christian education.

The *Broederbond*, which played a significant role in the 1930s as a secret Afrikaner nationalist 'shadow government', faded in influence after the National Party came to power. Such a man as T. E. Dönges wielded far more power as Minister of Finance than he ever had as a prominent *Broeder*. The organization has been kept in the public eye by rehashes of a handful of facts in overseas publications in the form of new *exposés* and by the circulation-building pull of 'Secret *Broederbond*' in the South African Sunday press. The vigilance of the latter is such that the *Broederbond* has not been able to hold a national meeting for years. Even plans for one soon leak to the press and the glare of publicity stops the meeting.

A difficulty with all secret organizations is how to wind them up when their function no longer exists. A great many, possibly a majority, of the leading members of the *Broederbond* have not had anything to do with it in years. Over a dozen *Broeders* have told the author that it has long outlived its usefulness – although discussion of it with an outsider is supposedly strictly prohibited. Where it continues to function is at a rather low level of 'jobs for pals' within the government and occasionally in contests for places on school boards and other local bodies. As a political force it is moribund but will continue to furnish eye-catching headlines.

From 1957 to 1961, there was a sharper separation into left and right wings of the dominant National Party. The old regional split of opinion between the Cape and the Transvaal again came to the fore. But throughout the country many ministers, professors, businessmen, and newspaper editors formed an intellectual minority for some liberalization of racial policies and were opposed by the vast majority of Afrikanerdom. Today, while liberal ideas inside Afrikaner nationalism are less well focused, they are diffused to more people than ever. The government's capture of the Afrikaner race relations university group known as S.A.B.R.A. in 1962, and the withdrawal of the Afrikaans Churches which had been in the World Council, are but two indications that liberal ideas crystallized in organizations are easy targets for the right wing. But at the same time, the seeds of non-racial ideas gain wider currency than ever among middle- and upper-class Afrikaners. Because of the danger to Afrikanerdom of allowing divergent parties, the one party remains, but covering broad differences of opinion.

The political push of the Republican Party or 'van der Merwe group' in the 1966 election is a manifestation of the right-wing sentiment for a return to baasskap (domination), but there was very little splitting of the nationalist vote. It is extraordinary that the Republicans could only gain 1 per cent of the vote by using the racialistic slogans of less than a decade ago, such as 'swart gevaar' ('black danger'), 'kaffir op say plek' ('native in his place') and 'baasskap' ('boss-ship'). As News/Check magazine (mildly sympathetic to the government at times) commented, 'The election showed how far the Afrikaner himself is aware that this election has shown how pointless some of the sacred slogans from the past have become.'[1] Editor Otto Krause's comments may be slightly more hopeful than descriptive but that this is the view of the former parliamentary correspondent of Die Vaderland is significant in itself. In a remarkable speech (reported privately to the author) in September 1966, a week before Verwoerd was assassinated, Nationalist M. P. Blaar Coetzee told an African audience in the Johannesburg township of Meadowlands that, 'We whites have trouble with agitators of our own who object to what the government has made available to Bantu in both homes and in schooling. We do not listen to their wicked language.' In an obvious reference to the van der Merwe/Republican

[1] Johannesburg, 8 April 1966.

right-wing splinter groups' failure in the 1966 General Election, Coetzee concluded that, 'in a recent election we rejected them with contempt.'

Also following the election, the student governing body of Stellenbosch University attacked Editor S. E. D. Brown of the far-right *South African Observer* for sowing disunity among Afrikaners by attacking leading Afrikaners for being 'liberalistic'. *Die Burger* and finally the then Verwoerd-controlled Afrikaans papers in the north joined the chorus of criticism against the extreme right.

Anomalously, a number of Afrikaner intellectuals have moved well to the left even of the opposition United Party, repugnant to many of them because of its alleged British 'jingoism', and, in the 1966 election, a hypercritical opportunism.

It is fair to say, although there are those who disagree, that Dr. Verwoerd began on the right wing of his Cabinet and over time moved almost to the left – especially in his emphasis on at least theoretically radical solutions. He held the Afrikaner right in tight control while constantly, especially after the Republic and military threats from Africa and abroad, drawing support from whites who were middle-of-the-road and, relatively speaking, to the left. In doing so, he went from almost no African support for the National Party in 1948 to, at a difficult estimate, perhaps 5 to 10 per cent of urban and perhaps as much as 20 to 25 per cent of rural Africans for some programme of separate development. The attendance at Verwoerd's funeral of Prime Minister Matanzima and his Cabinet was not so surprising, but the message of condolence from the Zulu Paramount Chief, Cyprian Bekuzulu, that 'We mourn the loss of a great statesman and friend who had at heart the welfare of all population groups and the Bantu in particular', spoke for more than a handful of sycophants. Cyprian is despised by African activists in South Africa and abroad, but he has by no means been wholly pliable in the hands of the South African government.

Prime Minister Vorster came to his leadership with nothing like the support Verwoerd ended with, but very much like the kind of support Verwoerd had when he started his premiership. Vorster started with the middle-right wing of his party staunchly behind him and the centre admiring his abilities. He did inherit a good deal of the growing English support Verwoerd had cultivated, and undoubtedly added a considerable support of his own arising from his successful suppression of sabotage. Coming in as Prime Minister, Vorster was almost unknown among Africans except as a symbol of the police and can have had only a microscopic following among Africans. It is a curious fact that among English-speaking South Africans, who have broadly liberal views, the coming to power of Malan was viewed at the time as Nazism triumphant. Then Malan was viewed more kindly when the 'terrible Lion of the North' Strijdom came to power. Whatever faults the latter had were in the liberal eye magnified many-fold by the advent of Verwoerd. Much of the same pattern was repeated with Vorster's taking over, except that some of the most pejorative descriptions had almost been exhausted and there was almost a nostalgia for Verwoerd among some of his severest critics at home and abroad.

Under Verwoerd, the National Party did not flaunt racist theories before the world as it once did. In practice, narrow financial self-interest has often carried more weight. Thus ideological pronouncements that Africans must be removed from certain parts of the Western Cape have been largely countermanded because of pressure from Afrikaner farmers. Likewise, the prospect of the removal of certain white traders from African reserves created white protest and a suspension of some steps towards removals. Middle- and lower-class Afrikaner groups have at last been able to gratify their wishes for higher levels of consumption.

Trade unions for Afrikaners with Nationalist goals took over from the relatively liberal British-oriented unions by 1955, and the contemporary issue has become social protection and not expansion. Despite substantial Afrikaner opposition inside the party and vociferous protests by workers of all races outside the National Party, a law to reserve (i.e., protect) jobs for members of a particular race (usually white) in such industries as the manufacture of clothing was passed and gingerly applied.

Rivalry among institutions is borne out most clearly in the Church–State split. Those to the right in the National Party claim that party pressure forced several churches out of the World Council of Churches, although other Afrikaners attribute the move to internal developments. Outspoken theological professors have been threatened with dismissal by the right-wing press, but there have been no actual dismissals reported. Relatively liberal Afrikaner *dominees* (ministers) have been fighting with some success, and those holding positions in various synods have been re-elected in the Cape and Transvaal as late as 1965.[1]

Afrikaners are far more world and Africa-conscious than ever before. This is at a time when the right wing of the National Party inveighs against foreign influence, especially American, whether it be in the form of publications, programmes for the exchange of persons, or even too much 'liberalism' in such staunch Afrikaner organs as the Prime Minister's *Dagbreek en Sondagnuus*, whose editor Dirk Richard came under attack by the far right in 1964 and after. Despite renewed anti-British feeling and considerable hostility towards the United States in the middle 1960s, highlighted by a series of unfortunate incidents, the broad thrust of Afrikanerdom has not been towards unrelieved isolationism. Senator Robert F. Kennedy was cheered by the Afrikaans students at Stellenbosch University when he spoke against isolationism, although the great majority were strongly opposed to many of his political views.

The reaching out of Afrikanerdom towards Africa is easily overlooked. South Africa was a leading member and valuable contributor to various co-operative scientific bodies until expelled by the new African states. But the change in attitude towards Africa and towards Africans in the last decade has been extraordinary. In 1955, the author talked at length about Africa with the late Prime Minister Dr. D. F. Malan. His hostility towards self-government for Ghana and the emergence of African states was almost matched by his real lack of knowledge of just where they were on the west coast and some of the elementary details of their development. He characterized his generation which knew far more of Europe than of Black Africa. In 1965, the author was again in Stellenbosch and had tea with Dr. Malan's widow: the subject

---

[1] Nevertheless, those 'liberal' Dutch Reformed Ministers who joined the oecumenical Christian Institute have been subjected to strenuous attacks in some of the Afrikaans press and have been rather isolated from the main body of the Nederduitsche Gereformeerde Kerk. The chief American editorializing on this issue has been the *Christian Century*. Unfortunately, this respected church journal has been rather consistently muddled in its comments. At one time or another, the *Christian Century* has said, for example, that Rev. Beyers Naude was tried for heresy in 1962 because of his attacks on the *Broederbond* – when he has never been tried for heresy and was re-elected Moderator of the Southern Transvaal Synod in 1963.

uppermost in Maria Malan's mind was a course she was taking on developing African countries.

In sum total, Afrikaner nationalism has not only passed through the middle and late stages of transition to full nationalism, but under the peculiar conditions of South Africa, it is on the verge of being submerged in a 'white nation' in the immediate future and eventually a multi-racial one. This 'white nation' now includes thousands of Italians, Germans, Dutchmen, Yugoslavs, Greeks, and other recent immigrants. Because 'English-speaking' whites feel compelled to seek shelter under the Afrikaner tent – even while some despise and bicker with their fellow occupants – this white *cum* white *cum* Coloured integration in the face of African nationalism foreshadows the end of exclusively Afrikaner nationalism. At the same time, it does not really create a total African nationalism, but further hardens the white *v.* black division.

THE BROADENING PARTY–'ENGLISH AFRIKANERS'

The 1960 referendum on whether or not South Africa should become a republic was a watershed in Afrikaner–English relations. Although the vote stirred up Tory ghosts of the Dominion Party among English-speaking people, and resurrected all the political shibboleths about Afrikaner nationalism, the referendum proved to have a cleansing influence on Afrikaner–English relations.

The initial reaction within the top ranks of both the United Party (U.P.) and the Progressives for an all-out fight against the republic was at best lukewarm. Of the individual leaders such as Sir de Villiers Graaff, Marais Steyn, Helen Suzman, or Jan Steytler, few had deeply emotional ties to Britain. Their strong sense of South Africanism reacted against an all-out fight. Later, the evidence piled up from the rank and file that anything less than total opposition to whatever had been proposed by the National Party would split the two opposition parties. It was particularly from the English-speaking stronghold of Natal that the most strident opposition was voiced as the Natal U.P. rallied round the Union Jack and, within party circles, insisted that the U.P. as a whole fight to the final whistle.

It is at least ironic that since the establishment of the Republic, by far the greatest gains of the National Party at the expense of the U.P. have been in Natal. This is further evidence of the purging of jingoistic feeling through the referendum. What finally convinced U.P. supporters in the Cape and Transvaal to fight South Africa's withdrawal from the Commonwealth were the economic arguments predicting catastrophic losses for Cape fruit farmers as well as a disastrous decline in general exports to Great Britain because of tariff changes. Even Cape Town's *Die Burger* shared some of the apprehension. When in fact the declaration of the Republic was followed by even greater trade with Great Britain and a generally booming economy, it was simplicity itself for those who had fought the Republic to forgive and forget. The faulty predictions of the economic Cassandras led many English-speaking people to sprinkle salt on some of the political criticism aimed at the National Party in the English-language press.

In the years following the establishment of the Republic the movement towards support of the National Party, if not Afrikaner nationalism, by more white South Africans has been encouraged by: (1) changes within Afrikanerdom, (2) changes inside African nationalism, (3) developments in Africa, and (4) the world scene.

The at least outward 'mellowing' of some aspects of Afrikaner nationalism was not lost on the whites outside it. During Verwoerd's leadership, Minister Albert Hertzog (son of the General), long a symbol of all the 'English' did not like, spoke less and less, and no longer in terms of the 'English' as enemies, while Verwoerd took the lead in conciliatory efforts. For example, the somewhat moribund *Broederbond* was given the task through its secretary (now M.P.) Piet Koornhof, of promoting cultural and institutional ties with the 'English'. Thus the *Federasie van Afrikaanse Kultuurvereniginge* (F.A.K.), the most Afrikaans of the in-groups, certainly ceased being actively anti-English and became even pro-English at times.

In the business world, the growing sophistication of Afrikaners and the bringing in of 'English' economists and businessmen to real government advisory positions, coupled with the dropping of ideas of nationalizing the gold mines, all built business confidence. Several broadly based and highly influential efforts were made to reach a public agreement between 'English' business and the government.

Although they did not succeed in their specific objectives, the efforts left a residue in 'English' minds that 'these Nats aren't so bad'.

It is difficult to assess how important to the changing attitude of English-speaking people was the appointment of Ministers Trollip and Waring. While as individuals they did not emerge as leaders of the 'English' within the government, they were certainly a prominent symbol and, in the case of Trollip, who had been a highly respected Administrator in Natal and proved to be a hard-working Minister of Labour, the impact on the English-speaking province of Natal was significant.

Much of the National Party advance in the province can be attributed to the policies of the Administrator, Theo Gerdener. As an Afrikaner heading an 'English' province, Gerdener gave the image of being the chief executive of a united province with a concern for the well-being of all its people. He did not indulge in harsh tirades against the predominant Zulu tribe, for example, but perhaps went farther than some previous Administrators in at least the formal respect he gave to Africans, Indians, and the small Coloured population. Whereas the Nationalist government had continually irritated Natalians with what they felt were Afrikaner pinpricks, Gerdener soothed feelings and avoided tension between the white groups. To be sure, one reason this was possible was a marked decline in English prejudice against Afrikaners. In an officially bilingual country, Durbanites had been taking offence in the 1950s at the growth of street signs in Afrikaans as well as English. There was also an arrogant unwillingness of English shop-girls to even attempt to speak Afrikaans with holiday-makers who began flooding down from the Transvaal and Orange Free State. This all changed in the 1960s, which meant that Afrikaners felt less pressure to push. However, it is doubtful if another Administrator than Gerdener would have been as successful.

The proof of a change in sentiment was evident not only at the polling-booths in Natal elections, but in the enthusiastic reception of Dr. Verwoerd on official visits to Durban after 1963. A decade earlier, only the then Foreign Minister, Eric Louw, would have been received with anything like genuine pleasure, and Dr. Verwoerd would have caused riots if he had done some of the things he did as a matter of routine on later visits to Durban.

Our second factor, changes in African nationalism, affected and continue to affect almost all white South Africans, but perhaps Natalians even more, because Natal has the largest rural and tribal concentration of Africans in the Republic. In the 1948 riot between Zulus and Indians, Durban had seen what an outbreak of violence might mean even if it had not then been directed at whites.

There are African nationalists and some white liberals who argue most forcefully that the leadership of the National Party has set a trap for English-speaking whites and that they have fallen into it. Part of the plan was the banning of African political organizations, not so much because they were a violent threat to the régime as to encourage or force them to take extreme stands and actions. Chief Luthuli had a considerable residue of white respect throughout South Africa until the period of Sharpeville and the burning of his pass. The growth of the 'Spear of the Nation', underground off-shoot of the African National Congress, the sabotage of the so-called 'African Resistance Movement' (A.R.M.) groups, and the statements by such men as Pan African Congress leader Leballo in Basutoland about the dire fate of white South Africans, all combined to force a choice.

Whatever latent sympathies many white South Africans may have had for African grievances were discouraged in the face of the alternative of violence, sabotage, and a planned overthrow of the government. Numerous liberals argue that the sequence of (1) government banning leading to (2) extreme African statements and white-led sabotage, leading to (3) English support of the National Party was, as suggested, a trap. If so, there are liberals who regret that many prominent members of the Liberal Party fell into the trap and alienated whatever hope they had for peaceful support from a broad cross-section of the white electorate. Those who chose violence were not all unaware of how their actions played into the hands of those Afrikaners who wanted the English in with them, but many concluded that the cause of peaceful persuasion was hopeless and that the sooner the next, if bloody, stage began, the sooner a resolution would come.

Developments in Africa as a whole, our third factor lending support to the National Party, have not been reported or interpreted in South Africa, even by the anti-government press, in such a way as to encourage English-speaking whites to gain confidence in African rule or even a shared rule. The Progressive loss has been the Nationalist gain, most notably in Natal in the 1966 election. In the process, the middle United Party has certainly picked up support from Progressive whites moving to the right but probably far less than it has lost by its own supporters swinging behind the Nationalists. The Congo disorders, East African mutinies, corruption followed by assassinations in Nigeria, attempts on Nkrumah's life and the coup against him, and clashing policies in North Africa, have all been played up far more than examples of racial trust and economic development. Communism in Africa was once an exclusive rallying cry of the National Party; however limited the actual impact, the subsequent efforts of the Chinese in Zanzibar, Burundi, Brazzaville, and in Lesotho, and of Cubans in Guinea and 'Brazza', have given weight to National Party predictions in the minds of many 'English' voters.

As for the fourth factor, the world scene has played into the hands of Afrikaner nationalism. On the one hand, the Soviet–American *détente* which might have led to stronger policies, even active co-operation, in southern Africa, became overshadowed by the rise of China as an atomic threat, the Viet-Nam war, United States troubles in Latin America led by the Dominican Republic, and the wrangling within the Common Market countries. The inactivity of the United Nations through 1964 was another factor. The West was in no mood or condition to unify with or without Soviet acquiescence. In the face of this inability or unwillingness to act against South Africa, the criticism levelled abroad at the Republic and reported – both sadly and gladly in the English press; sadly and defiantly in the Nationalist press – was felt by a wide cross-section of English-speaking whites to be unfair in the extreme. Strong but moderate criticism of South Africa was all but drowned out by the most extravagant language and strident tones of the most severe antagonists. The fact is that most white progressive leaders who tour the West, particularly the United States, are sometimes appalled at what they view as exaggerated and distorted attacks upon a government they sharply attack at home. When a graduate student in an African studies seminar in an American university accused the Progressive Party's lone parliamentary voice, doughty Helen Suzman, of being a 'fascist' because she demurred at some of the 'facts' in attacks on South Africa, she is reported to have said in a quiet voice,

'I'm not really a fascist or a Nazi but simply a Jewish girl from Johannesburg who is trying to uphold liberal principles.'

Whatever the actual merits or demerits of much overseas criticism, it appears immoderate and inaccurate to a substantial portion of the previously anti-National Party white electorate. If they did not like all features of Afrikaner politics, they liked foreign criticism and threats even less.

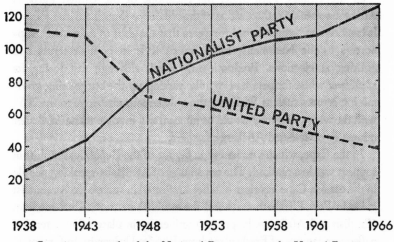

Growing strength of the National Party versus the United Party

Although the movement of so many English-speaking whites into the government camp can be explained by the factors we have considered, it does not follow that their actual entry has been an easy one. In fact, probably the greatest problem faced by the National Party in 1965 – a year when boycotts had dissipated, the South West Africa case at the World Court was still *sub judice*, and the economy booming – was how to absorb English-speaking support. No satisfactory answer was found.

In Natal, the large numbers of English supporters meant that party branches had an English flavour to them. There was almost no cultural shift. The language was the same as in the United Party and conservative U.P. supporters in the National Party felt a little more at home without a 'liberal' U.P. element to argue with in the party. Added to this was the anglicized nature of many of Natal's Afrikaners south of the traditional Nationalist strongholds such as Vryheid and Newcastle in northern Natal. There is no heritage of bitter local feuding between Englishmen and Afrikaner with the scars of a dozen past elections for the obvious reason that there were virtually no Afrikaners to fight. What scars do exist are from the Federal Party *v.* United Party provincial struggle of the 1950s and the Progressive *v.* United Party differences extending through the 1960s.

In the Orange Free State, the backbone of the United Party is Afrikaans-speaking, the residue of the old *Sappe* (South African Party). It has been so outnumbered for years that the shift of a few U.P. supporters to the Nationalist camp means little in popular terms and nothing at elections. Predominantly rural, although fast losing its *platteland* white farmers and rapidly picking up the burgeoning gold-mining centres such as Welkom, the only serious challenge to the N.P. with the white oligarchy would be internal and involve white Afrikaner miners or dissatisfied Afrikaner farmers.

In the Cape, which was barely in favour of the Republic, the shift in support was less marked. The percentage of Afrikaans-speaking people in the eastern Cape has risen and been reflected in successive Nationalist gains in Port Elizabeth seats and the establishment of a dual-medium (English and Afrikaans languages) university in place of an extension college or campus of English-medium Rhodes University in Grahamstown. The international-minded Afrikaner businessmen of Cape Town are acceptable to their English colleagues but do not proselytize them. Politics is altogether in a lower key. The tension which never dissipates for whites in Johannesburg because of the huge Soweto complex (the south-western townships for Africans) and the many thousands of Africans on the streets daily in the centre of the city, is absent from Cape Town. The whole Cape is further from Rhodesia and the Congo and likes to think of itself as more concerned with culture and less with the pressure of big business or big politics. Partly in reflection of this non-political *milieu*, there has been no great difficulty in the Cape in absorbing English supporters into the National Party, but they have been fewer.

The Transvaal is as different from the Cape as a giraffe from an antelope. In the rural areas, where at least the English-speaking farmer is *tweetalig* or bilingual and goes along with the whole conservative side of the United Party, a move from one party to another is not difficult beyond a matter of a few personal loyalties. It is somewhat harder for Afrikaner supporters of the United Party to make the change to the National Party because of the epithet so long hurled at them by National Party Afrikaners that they were *verraaiers* or traitors to Afrikanerdom.

In the middle-size towns which have been the swing seats from United Party to National Party in the last five elections – towns such as Boksburg, Germiston, Vereeninging, and, in 1966, Benoni and Springs – there are more difficulties. In Johannesburg and its peri-urban constituencies one finds very 'English' English people wanting to support the government who have never had close association with Afrikanerdom. A good many of them simply do not speak Afrikaans or not well enough to get by at meetings and to feel at home in conversation. At the same time, some of the Nationalist branches have the most Afrikaans, in a hard political sense, of Afrikaners to whom *die engelsman* was the sworn and bitter enemy. Nowhere else in South Africa do the Nationalists have the problem of trying to blend such diverse elements.

When the English-speaking support for the National Party was quite limited, it was easy to form a separate branch. The English-speaking John X. Merriman branch of the National Party is named after an honoured Cape politician-statesman. This concept of English branches has tended to break down for two reasons.

In the first place, the general composition of the Merriman branch contained a much higher proportion of *émigrés* from Eastern Europe than were found in the general English population. More European, deeply concerned with Communism as the chief enemy of South Africa, and some with a continental disdain for the British people, they were far from representative of either English-speaking farmers or businessmen. The right-wing proclivities of this non-British but English-speaking (in South Africa) minority in the National Party annoy not only some English but a good many Afrikaners who complain that they are 'more Nationalist than we are'. In the second place, as support has grown for the National Party, the natural desire of politically minded people to have a say in their own residential constituency came to the fore. The new English Nationalists were not used to sitting around coffee-houses and simply talking politics, but sought to work at it in their own communities.

Thus an effort was made in the early 1960s to integrate English and Afrikaner nationalists in local branches of the Witwatersrand. A further effort was the breakaway from separate minor publications for the separate English-speaking group, with the launching of a regular column in *Dagbreek en Sondagnuus* written by Blyth Thompson. This young English-speaking South African, who had put his energies into the real estate business in London, was aroused by the anti-South African campaign in Britain and soon headed an organization to counter-attack. Thompson toured the United States on a pro-South African speaking tour, subsequently moved to South Africa, and plunged into politics with the encouragement of the Prime Minister and other high Nationalist leaders. He had managerial and participant roles in English-language semi-political broadcasts from the South African Broadcasting Corporation. Finally, he stood for election for Johannesburg Northwest Rand seat as a Nationalist in the 1965 Provincial election and subsequently in South Coast, Natal, against U.P. Provincial Leader Douglas Mitchell, making substantial inroads into the solidly United Party and Progressive voting pattern of English-speaking voters in the 1966 General Election. Thompson, who had turned down what proved to be a winnable seat in Benoni, raised the National vote 600 per cent. Thompson is not alone among English-speaking Nationalists in looking towards a 'Third Force' of Natal and the Free State to hold a balance between the Cape and Transvaal.

The point of this somewhat detailed examination of the English swing to the National Party is that Blyth Thompson and others with him soon found that the National Party had great difficulty in absorbing them. Their support was welcome but not their ideas. Thompson's column was abruptly stopped because of some mild and indirect criticisms of policy – this view is disputed by well-informed people – although he continued to write in the Nationalist *Gazette* under a pseudonym. Intra-party rivalries and the long-standing mutual scrapping between the two language sections keep coming to the fore in the Transvaal. If the National Party becomes only 20 per cent English-speaking, this would be sufficient to drastically change many of the attitudes on which the party originally depended for unity. While not so in Natal, in the dominant Transvaal Afrikaner nationalism remains resistant to the pressure for a South African nationalism. The top leadership of the party in the Transvaal is committed to it. But the Nationalist Party is still very much a grass-roots organization. The usual United Party shibboleth that Nationalist voters are *skape* (sheep) being led to the polls had validity only when the choice was 'liberal English' rule versus Afrikaner *baasskap* (boss-ship) towards 'the natives'. Now that much of the United Party argument in the countryside aims to the political right of the National Party and attacks the Bantustan policy as being dangerously 'pro-Native', some of the old emotions have cooled and are replaced by newer issues. Thus the Nationalist leadership faces a twin problem: to break down the anachronistic *stryd tussen Boer en Brit stryheid* (struggle) within broader circles of its adherents, but to keep the party image far enough to the right to keep the United Party or the sporadic ex-Nationalist right-wing rebels from gaining mass support. Cabinet Minister P. W. Botha has frequently used in private an apt expression, in another context but it applies here: '*Ek praat regs sodat ek links kan doen*' ('I speak to the right [politically] so I can act to the left or liberal side').

If one assumes that the Bantustan policy and some present and more promised devolution of authority to Africans in the Transkei and else-where is 'liberal' when compared to *baasskap* policies, then it is probably a fair assessment that debated on this issue alone, it is very doubtful whether the National Party has the support of most of those who regularly vote for it at general elections.

Was the political story of Prime Minister Verwoerd in the 1960s that he pacified his 'left' by radical promises and then temporized in carrying them out because of an alleged fear of a 'right' revolt? Many Afrikaner observers thought just this, particularly those who have felt that the Prime Minister exaggerated the threat from his political right. And yet the story of Afrikaner politics has always been the outflanking of the leader from the right. Certainly the progression (or retrogression) north of the Limpopo, from Todd to Whitehead to Field to Smith, suggested to him that English-speaking whites in southern Africa might act along similar lines.

The germaneness of this to Afrikaner–English *toenadering* (getting together) is that Verwoerd may well have been building up an extra

G

dimension of political support for the deliberate day when the right wing of the party could be ignored and far more radical ventures than Bantustans embarked upon. Prime Minister Vorster pledged himself to Verwoerd's plans but execution in changed circumstances is always uncertain. For any Nationalist Prime Minister, the growing English support makes the task of an outside force wishing to split white South Africa much more difficult in the event of a showdown.

The author does not question that Dr. Verwoerd had a firm commitment to Bantustans. He often spoke – not for quotation – of both the moral and pragmatic need for an outlet for Bantu political aspirations. The lack of an outlet lay at the basis of his criticism – private, never public – of Rhodesian Front policies. He was the first South African Prime Minister who at least believed himself in a policy which he sincerely felt would in time provide an answer. Smuts's eyes were on such a distant horizon that his greatness on the international scene left him with feet of clay on 'native policy'. Neither Malan nor Strijdom had a final answer that did not always rest upon white power. It is extraordinary that Dr. Verwoerd was able to overcome much of his totalitarian image within South Africa and to gain a real measure of support for the Bantustan concept from generally liberally oriented people such as the editors of the *Star* and *Sunday Times* in Johannesburg, and even more liberal papers in the eastern Cape. What might have begun a real breakthrough in time began with the highly successful visit of Prime Minister Jonathan of Lesotho to Pretoria. All the hoary stories in the English press about Dr. Verwoerd being unwilling to shake the hand of a black man went up in smoke in the atmosphere of cordiality and promises of co-operation.

But whatever hard-won successes Verwoerd had with its critics outside the party, it is doubtful whether he ever convinced the rank and file within the National Party of the validity of the Bantustan concept. More than one Nationalist M.P. spoke privately of the Transkei as a smokescreen to deceive world opinion. And many who were impressed with Dr. Verwoerd's sincerity and tenacity became alarmed with the radicalness of a broader racial federation with a Transkei represented in the United Nations.

Therefore, Prime Minister Vorster in his early months had to face not only the question of how sincerely he might believe in 'separate development' beyond the sheer segregation stage, but also his own ability and power – initially far less than his predecessor and initially without a reputation for deep intellectual planning and logic – to carry on the Verwoerd programme he had formally pledged himself to follow.

Whereas Dr. Verwoerd, as we have discussed, had controlled the right, and Prime Minister Vorster should not have difficulties on that score, the more 'liberal' wing of Afrikanerdom which Verwoerd had finally placated and turned to supporters, will remain for a long time as a possible counterforce to Prime Minister Vorster. The new bridge to the 'English' which Verwoerd built is potentially a bridge to unite the relatively liberal whites within the strongly conservative, and at times afraid, white society.

If the National Party does embark on a more radical course than Bantustans, it will find enthusiastic support from its forward thinkers. *Burger* editor Cillie and *Beeld* editor Schalk Pienaar are only two of the more articulate of such Afrikaners. They complain that

... Afrikaners have often given the impression that they are in principle opposed to the liberation of all black people and thereby identified themselves with the outdated colonialism of Britain, France, Belgium and Portugal; but it was this same mentality that had opposed the Afrikaners' liberation.

Cillie and Pienaar recognize the parallel between Afrikaner and African nationalisms and that their Afrikaner principles 'are being used in our destruction'. Against this they prescribe that:

Old-time colonialist *baasskap* has not only become impractical in the modern world; nor does it only make our coexistence with other peoples impossible; we can no longer live with ourselves under such an order. ... We cannot and may not become the last fortress of a wrong order in the fighting against which the Afrikaner people were formed in a large degree.

To conclude our broad analysis of the course of Afrikaner nationalism to its final stage, it is wise to emphasize that many Afrikaners see the pattern as a different one than that portrayed here. For example, editor Willem van Heerden believes that this interpretation misses the significance of a broad South African nationalism as featured by General Hertzog's efforts to unite the white groups over a span of forty years. Van Heerden also believes that English and Afrikaans differences have been grossly exaggerated so as to pass over a greater national sentiment preached by Hertzog and promoted by Prime Minister Verwoerd with remarkable success. This view of a broader white nationalism, which would include black nationalism, is a vision held by a handful of influential Afrikaner thinkers through the decades. However, it is difficult for the author to reconcile such views with the widespread and bitter feelings held by Afrikaners and English-speaking South Africans about each other, when the author first visited South Africa in 1949 after the Nationalist Victory of 1948. The 'enemy' was the other white group and 'race relations' were popularly defined as being English and Afrikaner relations. It was the lack of African power – through tribes, Bantustans, or mass movements in modern dress – to influence the affairs of government, which left only the Afrikaans and English-speaking whites in the political arena to punch each other and build up enmities. This preoccupation with 'white' politics, even though Africans were a pawn in that struggle, underlies the reason why there has been a general failing in South Africa to come to grips with the basic political facts of a country four-to-one African.

CHAPTER VII

AFRICAN NATIONALISM – TO THE MIDDLE STAGE

EARLY STAGE

The early stage of African nationalism had its roots in tribally based opposition to the successive encroachment of whites as they settled north and east of the Fish River. The famed Zulu warrior Dingaan fought the Boer *Voortrekkers* as his predecessors had fought, and all but destroyed numerous African tribes. Dingaan wished not only to defend 'his country' but to add vast dominions to it. But his bloodthirsty actions should not obscure the thousands of small and unsung instances when Africans lost their land by fair means (in white eyes) through forms of purchase or simply were driven from it. The long series of intermittent 'Kaffir Wars' fought by British troops (including Hessian mercenaries) are comparable to the engagements of the U.S. Army against the American Indians. The justification in both countries included retaliation for cattle-raiding, isolated murders of settlers, and the use of European 'legal' documents all to the end result of depriving the weaker tribes of their land. The slaughter in South Africa was less but the moral issues were the same. The long history of the Bastards under Adam Kok, a Coloured community with the rudiments of Western living patterns, is tragic evidence of the drive by Afrikaners and English on the frontier.

Following the wholly tribal phase, a sense of African nationalism emerged from the upper class of Westernized Africans. It gained momentum after the turn of this century and continued with growing strength until well after the Second World War, when the intermediate stage began. Charisma was of great importance in the early stage. Individuals stand out more than organizations. In literature, it was Sol T. Plaatje who wrote widely and translated classics such as

Shakespeare's *Julius Caesar* into Tswana. In the 1920s, Plaatje partially supported a tour of the United States by selling over 18,000 copies of a pamphlet, *The Mote and the Beam*, setting out the case of Africans as they saw the 'white peril'. Plaatje felt a great need to provide an account of history in South Africa through African eyes. His historical novel *Mhudi*[1] is an account of African life and encounters with the Europeans in the 1830s.

In this early stage of African nationalism, most of the leadership had been mission-trained. This not only contributed to a peaceful expression of grievances, but also tended to set off many of the leaders as part of the small Christian upper class separate from what were commonly viewed as the raw, ignorant, and pagan minority. This generation felt the grievances of the past in rational, not irrational, ways, with charity rather than hate, in sadness more than anger, and in hope rather than cynicism. Plaatje's dedication of a book, 'To the memory of OUR BELOVED OLIVE, one of the many youthful victims of A SETTLED SYSTEM', shows a historical awareness of some of the forces which led to his daughter Olive's death from influenza at thirteen, but it expresses pathos rather than bitterness.

Out of a similar *milieu* came newspaper editor John Tengo Jabavu, who founded *Imvu Zabantsundo* (Native Opinion). The Jabavus are one of the distinguished families of South Africa. The editor's son, D. D. Jabavu, was a Professor at Fort Hare College, and today his granddaughter, Noni, has written books and edited a literary magazine in London before moving to Jamaica.

In Chapter I reference was made to a South African with great personal flair and a genius for leadership, Clements Kadalie, who founded the Industrial and Commercial Workers' Union of Africa (I.C.U.). Originally it sought to organize dock workers, but gradually became the most important African union with numerous successes and a fairly broad national support.

Kadalie, who came from Nyasaland, was well aware of the broader African complaints. His exposure of ills led the London *Times* to exclaim, 'The genuine grievances of the South African Natives provided the hot-bed in which the I.C.U. flourished. Rack-rented Natives in the urban locations, underpaid Natives in Government

[1] Lovedale Press, 1930.

employ, badly treated Natives on European farms flocked to join the movement.'

Kadalie had many problems – organization problems and also a lack of strong lieutenants. The implacable white opposition was possibly too much for any such organization at that period of South African history. When the I.C.U. tried to invade the Orange Free State, there were riots. His African organizers were killed – five on one occasion in Bloemfontein. Strong opposition from the white government was a major factor in the eventual demise of the I.C.U. in the middle 1920s. But it was not only outside his organization that he had problems with whites, for Kadalie was only the first of many African nationalist leaders to be 'white-anted' from within. Most of the whites who are prominent in the higher circles of African nationalism in South Africa, throughout its history right up to the present day, have been members of the Communist Party. At an I.C.U. meeting in Port Elizabeth, Kadalie came to a showdown with his unwanted white Communist allies. To keep the Communists out, Kadalie tried a tactic which was later to be emulated by the Pan African Congress in the 1950s; he opposed all participation by all white people. He spoke volubly from the platform to his African supporters: 'What do you Natives want with Communism? You want more wages, better conditions, repeal of pass laws, etc., not Communism, the meaning of which 65 per cent of you don't know.' Kadalie won that fight, but he was a lone leader and his magnetic qualities could not substitute for the bricks and mortar of a continuing movement.

In addition to being confined to the *élite*, of which Kadalie was only one, African nationalism fits the model of the early stage by being only partially revolutionary, emphasizing charisma or magical leadership qualities; having a platform of general grievances with a broad appeal to diverse African groups; but leaving the broad mass of Africans untouched, and featuring a drive of upward mobility on the part of many Africans.

African nationalism came to its mimetic phase at almost the same period we have discussed in Afrikaner nationalism. Although parts of the leadership did become as deeply or more deeply involved with a foreign ideology, in neither nationalism did grass roots exist for an imported ideology.

Does ideology or race dominate the reaction against Afrikaner Nationalism? The answer revolves around crucially 'modern' African leaders, and particularly the intellectuals in exile, who are diametrically opposed to the interpretation of African nationalism as the Afrikaners see it. Many intellectuals among the Afrikaners prefer to think overwhelmingly in ethnic terms and of tribal or group interests corresponding to sub-racial interest groups among the whites. Bantustans for rural areas and 'ethnic grouping' in white urban areas are based upon this assumption. Such a view can be over simplified. On the other hand, the interpretation of articulate African intellectuals that African nationalism became ideological rather than tribal, especially after 1935, is not the whole story. It is critical to an understanding of African nationalism to understand how African intellectuals interpret its development. Let us therefore attempt to summarize the sequence of events as they occurred and are interpreted by sophisticated Africans and many liberal whites.

In their view, the take-off point was Prime Minister Hertzog's Natives Representation Bill of 1935. Prior to that the hope, however delayed, was for a gradually spreading African franchise based upon British anticipations at the time of Union. But Hertzog removed Cape Africans from a common voters' roll and replaced this politically with the scheme for three white representatives to be voted upon by African males (still only in the Cape Province) in the House of Assembly. Provision was also made for a Natives Representative Council which was in a sense the forerunner of the present Transkei legislature.

African resistance to this change in the political pattern was strong in the urban areas. The All-African Convention was created as a federation of African political, educational, business, and cultural groups. The task of the A.A.C., under its first President Professor D. D. T. Jabavu, was to 'render all segregatory legislation unworkable'. In 1936 the A.A.C. was widely accepted by urban Africans as the 'political mouthpiece of the African people'. The African National Congress and the Communist Party (numerically unimportant) supported it at that time. In 1943 the A.A.C. embarked on a policy of 'non-collaboration' defined as 'complete rejection of all political institutions created for an inferior people'. Neither the African National

Congress nor the Communist Party joined this crusade. It would have meant the withdrawal from Parliament of the white Communist representatives such as Sam Kahn. Young African National Congress members fought for non-collaboration, but many older A.N.C. members who belonged to the Native Representative Council refused to resign, claiming that they would 'fight segregation from within'.

The position of the All African Convention was, it is quite evident, ideological as well as tactical. It also applied to the opposition. At this stage of South African history – the 1940s – the mass recruitment of Africans to urban areas during the war and after was just under way and much of the political focus remained on the Cape, where Africans had held and still held more political rights. It is therefore significant that the politics of the Coloured community, so important numerically in the western Cape, became entangled with African politics as the movement of Africans into the western Cape grew in significance. African reserves, with their tribal basis of organization, and the unorganized African labourers on white farms, were not in the political picture.

In a move not unlike that regarding Africans' representation in 1935, the Smuts government created a Coloured Affairs Department in 1943 and a Coloured Advisory Council paralleling the Native Representative Council. The reaction in the Cape was strong among a militant section of the generally apathetic Coloured community and the 'Anti-C.A.D.' movement was founded. Without digressing to a detailed discussion of the many intricacies of Coloured politics, what is significant is that the Anti-C.A.D. and the All African Convention created a super federation known as the Non-European Unity Movement. The new-born N.E.U.M. anticipated that an Indian group would be formed to join with it but this never materialized. Its whole approach was to have nothing to do with government efforts to organize ethnic groups along ethnic lines. It had a non-racial ideology. In time it broke down because it was so utterly negative in its approach that those who wanted either action against the white government or collaboration with it, had no place. Many of the Coloured supporters were teachers and a policy of political non-activity allowed them to keep their jobs and salve their consciences. A significant number of them were Trotsky-oriented in opposition to the Stalinist Communist Party.

The foregoing interpretation of the period from 1935 to 1950 does show a non-racial dimension and an ideological emphasis which is looked back upon with pride and emotion by those Africans and Coloured participants who were involved. But by 1950 the weight had shifted to the Transvaal in non-white as it had in white politics, and a schism developed between the Coloured and African political groupings. It is since 1960 that ethnic considerations have re-emerged in African politics. This parallels the transition from a relative handful of westernized Africans meeting and planning together on a fairly informal and democratic basis in a few big metropolitan centres, to the last decade in which many of the 'reserves' have become politically conscious and the numbers of urban Africans have become much larger.

Returning to the present, there is a factor in African nationalism which did not exist for Afrikaner nationalism – namely a nationalist leadership abroad. Unless you include the leadership of the two northern republics as sources of inspiration for Afrikaners left behind in the Cape, Afrikanerdom has never taken direction from leaders outside its geographical boundaries. It is true that small groups of Afrikaners settled abroad after the defeat of the Boer War. But neither from Kenya, where some of them trekked to, nor from South America, where more went and were more successful, was there leadership to continue the fight. Embittered individuals who went into exile never played a role in turning the tides of Afrikaner fortunes.

Leadership of African nationalism in South Africa exists both within the country and abroad in pluralistic variety. The differences are so great that it might be more correct to talk of African nationalisms.[1] One important complicating factor is that whenever a South African

[1] The tribal origins of the African population according to the 1960 census were as follows:

Xhosa	3,423,000	Tsonga	366,000
Zulu	2,959,000	Swazi	301,000
Northern Sotho	1,122,000	Venda	195,000
Southern Sotho	1,089,000	Southern Ndebele	162,000
Tswana	863,000	Northern Ndebele	47,000
		Other	280,000

Needless to say, in a number of instances the whole tribe is much larger in number, such as the Swazis, of whom a majority live outside South African boundaries.

African leader goes abroad into voluntary or forced exile, his influence drops within the country. New leaders arise even under the closest police surveillance. As the difficulties multiply for those who organize within the country, so do the difficulties for those who would see their leadership penetrate into South Africa from without. A concomitant of this is the difficulty in knowing who is a leader – external or internal.

Despite greater education, higher incomes, more urbanization, and deeper grievances, African nationalists in the Republic have lagged politically behind their contemporaries elsewhere on the continent. One reason is not far to seek: stringent laws backed by a powerful police force and army. One must also include, seemingly paradoxically, the higher material standard of living achieved by successive African generations in the Republic. After the famous American Negro actor, Canada Lee, visited various African political leaders in 1949 during the filming of *Cry, the Beloved Country*, he exclaimed to the author, 'They never had it so good and they are afraid to die.' In a sense, the material advances of Africans in the Republic both postpone and make inevitable voluntary changes. They will not all come together, or necessarily be only political. The last decade has seen sensational changes in some areas of African employment.

As models for African nationalism, three possibilities suggest themselves: democracy, Communism, or 'African socialism'. 'Neutralism' is an African – and Asian – created stance which may or may not be adopted *after* a nationalistic movement has succeeded. As such it has limited interest for Africans in the Republic at this stage. African socialism is more often applauded in independent Africa than defined. 'Nkrumahism' was one version, but each country paying some lip-service to 'African socialism' has its own interpretation. It is not as yet a full philosophical model. The preferred choice in South Africa is very clearly Western democracy. In this decision Africans are deeply influenced by the Western *milieu* within which nearly all their leaders have been forged. For decades the Africans have overheard the Afrikaner cries for political rights and for fair treatment in the market-place by English-speaking whites. On every hand Western democracy is extolled as the ideal, and in nearly every English-language newspaper Africans are told that Afrikaners do not practise it, and that if they did Africans would reach some of their cherished goals.

But the techniques of Western democracy for gaining power such as political parties, electoral campaigns, and ultimately the ballot box, have never been freely offered to Africans in South Africa and are almost non-existent for them today. In the compromise of Union, the British government agreed to the exclusion of African voters from the common political roll outside the Cape Province. The British had hoped that the example of the Cape would extend to the other three provinces. Instead these rights were withdrawn in 1936, and in 1959 even representation of 9,000,000 Africans by three white M.P.s was ended. The trade unions as vehicles for political pressure are also effectively closed to Africans by discriminatory legislation. It is clear that any normal avenue of peaceful political expression common to the democracies of Western Europe which Africans might adopt, would be summarily closed to them by legislation and, if unwilling to accept this peacefully, by force. It is, of course, true that political change in nearly all of Africa is barred by force and is not available through the ballot box.

The reaction has been a trend towards Communist leadership of African nationalism. Thus the general strike of 31 May 1961 was led by three militant Marxists and former (if not present) adherents of the Communist Party of South Africa. Although this general strike failed, and the overall African leadership is by no means Communist, the trend is in that direction. The practice by many Afrikaner politicians of labelling almost all African nationalism as 'Communist' went a long way towards building up an image of 'Communism' as a desirable ally in the minds of Africans, although the purpose was to influence the leaders of the West in order to draw their political and military support. The writer encountered an amusing twist in Windhoek, South West Africa, from African labourers who had gone to Walvis Bay to see the Soviet fishing fleet calling there. They returned surprised that the people the South African government was so against and afraid of were not 'black' but 'white'.

Communism would seem, on the face of it, to have a great potential appeal to the ill-informed African mass. The reported economic achievements of some Communist countries can be held up as inspirational models for African nationalists. But whatever the potential appeal Communism has had, realization has never been approached.

The Communist Party has had pitifully few successes since 1922, when white miners went to the scaffold singing 'The Red Flag'. Ironically, it was the song of anti-black Communism, for that party's greatest appeal in South Africa has always been to white citizens. Today it attracts the anti-racist sections of whites and, since 1950, also a group of Indian intellectuals.

The dependence in the early stage upon foreign example provided an early opening for Communism. Probably the first African Communists from South Africa to make important visits to Moscow were Laguma and Gumede. The latter had been President of the African National Congress when they attended the tenth celebration of the October Revolution. The slogan adopted at that time has anachronistic phrasing, but it provided a clear-cut goal: 'An independent South African Native Republic is a stage towards the workers' and peasants' republic with full safeguards and equal rights for all national minorities.'

The Communist Party never exceeded a membership of 1,500 while it was legal, and of this number fewer than a quarter were Africans. Although the Stalinist purge of the white Communist leadership in the 1930s represented an attempt to shift South African leadership from white to black hands, it was premature and wrecked the party organization. Otherwise Communism could have gained ground in the great depression, and really made strides when Soviet military efforts in the Second World War were earning the plaudits of the South African press.

For a generation most African nationalist leaders have fought against Communist infiltration. In considering Communism as a possible model, Africans in the Republic have been so concerned with the efforts of local white Communists to infiltrate African nationalism with the aid of African allies, that the African nationalist leadership has never been able to raise its eyes to the world level to judge – for good or evil – the possibility of Communism as a model.

Until just recently, all potential Communist-model nationalisms were white and European, a severe handicap in an atmosphere of white *v.* black. Racially mixed parties at the Soviet Legation during the Second World War did erase certain doubts, but since the expulsion of the Soviet representatives from South Africa in 1956 the image of Communism as being 'white' has grown.

Whereas the old Communist Party was interracial, the successor 'Congress' movement is racially segregated. In contrast, the tiny, racially integrated Liberal Party of South Africa says it is anti-fascist, anti-Communist, and anti-*apartheid*. The white members of the old Communist Party belong to and dominate the now almost extinct Congress of Democrats (C.O.D.), a lily-white organization. The C.O.D. was the leader of the Congresses. These have included a weak Coloured Congress (with a white president), the strong Indian Congress, a weak trade-union Congress (S.A.C.T.U.), and the African National Congress. The banned and underground African National Congress (A.N.C.) has been by far the largest Congress unit and has the only independent personality. The C.O.D. from time to time manipulated the upper echelons of the A.N.C., sometimes by the simple means of giving a hungry man a job at £20 per month. But it failed in its efforts to extend to the grass roots – white or black.

Nevertheless, in a reaction against what some Africans, and especially the youth section of the A.N.C., felt was Communist influence in the A.N.C., along with a strong feeling that the A.N.C. 'wasn't delivering the goods', the Pan Africanist Congress (P.A.C.) was formed in 1958. It made rapid headway and was overtaking the A.N.C. in influence when its anti-pass campaign came to a bloody end in the March 1960 Sharpeville massacre. Was the Pan-Africanist reaction against the A.N.C. more anti-white or more anti-Communist? It is difficult to judge. The dominant sentiment varies from one P.A.C. member to another. Because the 'outsiders' allegedly manipulating the A.N.C. were both white and Communist, the question is not fully answerable.

The foregoing outline explains in part the focus of attention within African nationalism upon Communism inside South Africa, and why Communism outside is scarcely considered as a matrix on which to pattern African nationalism. Thus African nationalism in the Republic lacks a strong model, for even though Marxism has little attraction, liberalism too will be ineffective so long as the ends of the Western democracy remain divorced from the means of reaching them. In general, the A.N.C. wants full rights for all South African citizens, and the P.A.C. wants 'Africa for the Africans', without specifying whether this adage means expulsion of or co-operation with Europeans,

Indians, and Coloureds. But in any case, the P.A.C. desires Western democracy for Africans, even though under prevailing conditions Communist techniques have sometimes been adopted as a means of reaching Western democratic goals. Inconsistencies must clearly arise to make this curious marriage unstable, and the possibility that Communist means will lead to Communist ends is obvious.

Without further recapitulating the history of the Communist Party of South Africa, suffice it to say that by 1966 its membership stood at about 700, with possibly another 6,000 sympathizers. Fragmentation of the African nationalist movement inside the Republic makes it difficult to estimate the degree of Communist control today, but it has increased in the underground as legal and police pressures have become more effective. Since 1962 the Communist Party and the African National Congress have co-operated in the sabotage organization, 'Spear of the Nation'.

Ideologically, the Communist African elements within the African nationalist movements continue to look to the Soviet Union as a model rather than to the People's Republic of China or a Titoist form such as Yugoslavia.

Foreign and domestic models for politically conscious non-Communist Africans – an overwhelming majority of the African nationalists as a whole – have undergone a shift since the Second World War. The British model and practice was not only the best known, but almost the only model perceived by all except a handful of the intelligentsia. Africans had started on the path followed by Africans in other territories associated with Great Britain. Their hopes were that the franchise would be broadened beyond the adult male Africans of the Cape Province to all of South Africa and, more importantly in terms of political power, that there would be an increase in the number of parliamentary seats from three to something equal to or approaching the African percentage of the population. The hope flickered through the 1920s and 1930s, and went out with the accession to power of the Afrikaner Nationalists in 1948. For a while there was faith in the United Party which, despite its discriminatory legislation, had at least paid lip-service and made some minor concessions to African political aspirations. These hopes died as the United Party moved to the right or, more accurately, appeared to move to the far right in African terms when compared to the sweeping enfranchisement of millions of Africans throughout the continent and the independence of most African states.

Although the Liberal Party held out a non-racial torch, it shed a very small light for Africans, and outside a limited number in urban townships and in the Transkei, few of them saw it at all.

The Progressive Party came on the scene at a time when it was apparent to most observers that the British parliamentary pattern was not going to develop and upper-class Africans were already frustrated and sour. African attitudes towards 'white' thinking had been curdled by successive Nationalist legislation which the Africans saw as putting one man–one vote out of reach. This is not to say that the vast majority of Bantu-speaking people in the Republic would not welcome the accession of the Progressive Party to power. But the unlikelihood of this happening, plus the disenchantment with peaceful means of action by a militant minority, has led Africans to leave the Progressives as a 'white' party with Coloured additions. This analysis of their party is accepted by most Progressive leaders as a reasonable African conclusion at this time. Indeed, a split in the Progressive hierarchy after 1963 has been over the issue of recruitment of Africans. M.P. Helen Suzman has held that Africans respect power and that the 'Progs' should strive to win parliamentary seats within the white electorate so that they have some actual strength when they ask for African support. Others in the Progressive Party would rather downgrade the parliamentary effort to build a broadly based non-racial party. The choice is a real one in that the time, money, and energy put into a political meeting or a *huisbesoek* (house-visiting or door-to-door canvassing) campaign among Africans means one less speech or campaign among the white electorate. The Suzman analysis is probably the correct one because there is little patience among urban Africans for 'tea-party' meetings which produce some racial goodwill but have no prospect of real action. This the Progressives acknowledge but perservere in the belief – or hope – that a time will come when both white and black will rally to their principles.

The number of Africans who turned to the Soviet Union as a model has been, as discussed, quite limited in numbers. It was the emergence of the United States as a world power after the Second World War which created a new model for African nationalism. It was not that the

American principles, as Africans saw them, were so significantly different to those of Great Britain, but that they had a strong rebirth on the world scene. The United States as a model had the great attraction because 10 per cent of its people were of African origin, and it included a theory and a principle of equality of races under a common flag. The United States held the great disadvantage that segregation by law in the South and *de facto* in the North was well-known to African newspaper-readers in South Africa. However, the U.S. Supreme Court decision on school segregation was a bombshell in South Africa – to both whites and blacks – and was discussed and argued about in African nationalist circles. The author was in Cape Town at the time, and vividly recalls the shouts of the Coloured newsvendors and the excitement as people of all races bought papers with the latest news. The polarization of the cold war between Moscow and Washington also exerted an influence in model-selection. African nationalists inclined to favour Moscow introduced the first really bitter anti-American feeling among Africans in the Republic. This was abetted in the Communist press, such as *New Age*, with the usual stories about lynchings in the American South, germ warfare in Korea, and the new American imperialism in Africa. The very antipathy for the U.S. in the more left-wing African circles tended to push Africans, who were not so inclined, towards the United States. This tendency has continued to the present day. Links with the American Negro community, dating to the nineteenth century, have tended to provide American Negro heroes for the pantheon of the new model.

But before the American model began to displace the British one, something which was never completed, the emergence of independent African states complicated the quest for an ideal. Ghana stood high on the horizon before many Africans from the Republic had visited there. It is true that individual African leaders such as His Imperial Majesty Haile Selassie, Sékou Touré, and Jomo Kenyatta are well-known through mass circulation magazines and are an inspiration to young African nationalists. But on a more sophisticated level, the coolness so often existing when African leaders from the Republic seek employment or refuge elsewhere in Africa becomes a barrier. Even in their state of relative weakness and lack of political power, many African leaders in the Republic (and those in exile from the Republic) consider

H

their political abilities superior to those found in most African states. Abroad they are sometimes painfully ambivalent about the 'superior' African Westernized society of Johannesburg compared to the lesser developed capitals of black Africa. Their love for South Africa in a physical sense and their pride in mastering a society of skyscrapers and steel-mills, to which they have contributed so much, are in conflict with their intense emotion over their lack of success in achieving their political goals.

This evaluation of foreign models and domestic political parties would be incomplete if one did not emphasize the broad liberal education of many thousands of Africans without any taint of Communism. Most of such education has come through Christian schools in both the cities and the reserves. For example, Nelson Mandela was educated by South African missionaries. One of his former teachers has described to the author how Mandela, along with many compatriots, came into association with Communists after his adolescent years. This prominent liberal says very frankly that, in the A.N.C., 'I think the Communist influence was very strong and skilled but few Africans accepted its theory as practice.' It has long been the charge of Afrikaner nationalists that while many missionaries have been and are pro-Christian and anti-Communist, their liberal teachings produce excellent material for Communist recruitment. The rejoinder is usually that if this is true the responsibility rests upon a system of discrimination which embitters such Africans. Prime Minister Verwoerd's answer to that charge was to cite it as a fundamental reason for the need of separate development. What can be confidently asserted is that the great majority of those Africans attracted to modern political movements in key cities have had little real knowledge of Marxism and have not been attracted to it; that the issue is whether or not a dedicated and clever Communist minority of the leadership has, with white Communist assistance, been able to manipulate a larger urban group primarily concerned with social and economic grievances.

Since the launching of the Transkei government in 1961, a new alternative model has been offered in the package labelled 'separate development'. This was much scorned by professional social scientists, nearly all of them strongly anti-*apartheid*, both in and out of South Africa. Predictions of its complete failure with Africans were commonplace in the years after it was announced. The assassination of Prime Minister Matanzima was predicted along with the complete rejection of any *modus vivendi* with the present South African government.

It is still true that nowhere in South Africa have a majority of adult Africans voted for a system of 'separate development'. The ruling party in the Transkei stands for such a policy, but depends upon the votes of nominated chiefs for its parliamentary majority. However, the present stage in the Transkei is far from the 'fraud' it is sometimes described as being by the more severe critics of the South African government. It does follow very closely the long-established British practice of beginning democratic rule with a majority of nominated members. In the Transkeian Legislature chiefs are nothing like a majority. If a majority of Africans in each constituency voted against the separate development party candidate, there would be no majority of the Matanzima party as it presently exists. In the five years of trial, it has clearly been demonstrated that some Africans in the traditional reserves, as well as in the large urban townships, profess to believe in a general policy of separate development along the general lines initiated by Verwoerd when he was a Cabinet Minister and in his tenure as Prime Minister either as a matter of principle or of expediency. It is significant that politicians sympathetic to separate development attract their greatest support when they press the South African government. This needling and demanding of more and more rights within the framework of separate development is likely to increase. Indeed, it is the prospect of an independent Transkei with an Ambassador at the United Nations which provided the United Party with a bogey man to frighten the white voters of South Africa to vote the 'radical' Dr. Verwoerd out of power if they were to save their white skins. The same line of political attack would probably not have been used if Mr. Vorster had been Prime Minister at the time of the 1966 election.

Despite the proliferation of models from Great Britain, the Soviet Union, the United States, new African states, and the Transkei as part of separate development, there remains in African nationalism the platform of general grievances with a broad appeal.

But Western parliamentary democracy in a unified state or Communism are not workable models in the present environment. Younger but more rapidly successful African nationalist movements elsewhere on the continent are powerful incentives, but somewhat vague examples for practice. African nationalists who leave the Republic, usually covertly, find great stimulus in association with nationalists elsewhere in Africa, but they quickly lose much of their influence inside South Africa. Passive resistance was an import of the early 1950s. It came from India and was taught to African nationalists by the Indian National Congress of South Africa, although it was Mohandas Gandhi who worked out the principles of his methods in South Africa in pre-First World War days, before launching his ideas in British India. Today boycotts are influenced from abroad, although the germ has never died in South Africa since the days of Afrikaner boycotts of British traders in the early stages of their nationalism.

Among African nationalists, there is precious little to be loyal to except rather vague organizational names. Slogans and symbols do have a broad identification. These are most common in the cities, but in the rural *kraals* (villages) in the late 1950s one also saw pennants denoting allegiance to a political movement. The Minister of Justice received power to ban symbols, and posters and the writing of slogans on walls or buildings is now subject to heavy penalties. Efforts of African nationalist leaders to promote boycotts and strikes have repeatedly broken down in their inability to transform a strong but unorganized loyalty into concrete action. In general, only when it is backed by an economic grievance (a penny rise in the bus fares has served effectively) or a sharp emotional issue (the 'massacre' at Sharpeville) is this loyalty crystallized.

African respect for the laws of the land has been eroded on every hand. The public demonstrations of burning the hated 'pass books' by otherwise law-abiding and staunchly Christian Africans is at one end of the scale. At the other end are the savage and sometimes orgiastic assaults upon the enemy, whether they be police or innocent bystanders such as a white nun. One of the few deaths in the 1960 Langa (Cape Town) riots occurred when the Coloured driver for the anti-*apartheid* *Cape Times* was dragged out of a reporter's car and set on fire. A police uniform, whether worn by an African or an Afrikaner, is an object of hate to many and of respect to few. But respect for the symbols and leaders of African nationalism is widespread.

At the end of the Second World War, large masses of the African population scarcely felt the wind of nationalism, a fact true today only in limited rural areas. In the cities, broad support can be obtained for highly specific short-term goals or grievances. A bus boycott supported by the African National Congress will succeed as it did in 1947 and in subsequent years, whereas work boycotts may fail as in 1958 and 1961. In the former, men were asked to contribute a long walk to work and back, while in the latter they were expected to forgo the money they and their families needed.

Strong desires for upward mobility in the small African middle class are intensified by restrictions imposed from outside African society. As a consequence, instead of some middle- and upper-class Africans being lost by assimilation into the traditionally ruling group of Afrikaners, virtually all such Africans are frustrated and fortified in their demands for the redress of all wrongs done to Africans.

Charisma is of supreme importance in the legitimization of African leadership. The government contributes to this personalism by banning political organization and imprisoning leaders, a policy which tends to make African nationalism a body without a head and consequently unpredictable at times. It was an ideal environment for an individual to rise to great, if brief, power through his charismatic qualities. For example, one Phillip Kgosana was a quiet and essentially passive college student, with an unusual naïveté for his twenty-one years. Yet his influence skyrocketed so in a few short months that in March 1960 he marched into the centre of Cape Town with upwards of 5,000[1] African demonstrators behind him. In his open-necked shirt, blue shorts, and sandals, he parleyed with nervous police officials. When he was satisfied, he ordered the huge African throng to return peacefully to their homes some twelve miles away. They obeyed him. His hold on them, now long dissipated, was astonishing. The government has now gone beyond banning organizations – a step which favoured the charismatic rise of the single individual – to placing controls on individuals the moment they begin to attract any following.

Neither of the most publicized leaders today – Nelson Mandela of the African National Congress nor Robert Sobukwe of the Pan Africanist Congress – has a chance to demonstrate his own charismatic powers. Both are imprisoned on Robben Island in Table Bay, although

[1] Some observers claim 20,000.

Sobukwe has long since served his sentence and is detained under special powers granted the Minister of Justice. Those of his friends who visit him remark on Sobukwe's general health, prevalence of books and gramophone discs, and time for study under general detention. Mandela had a 'fling' at the Rivonia Trial and made an eloquent statement of his beliefs. When he was given life imprisonment instead of the possible death sentence, he became less a rallying point overseas.

Although Sobukwe's tactics in the 1960 heyday of the Pan Africanist Congress were 'No bail; no defence; no fines', thus having himself and all his protesting followers go to jail, his years in prison may have modified his thinking. In 1964, he applied to the government for an 'exit permit' to leave South Africa, on condition that he could not return. Some of his followers were sharply critical of him for this. The government gave the request considerable thought. In the end, officials were privately sceptical of whether Sobukwe would stay out of politics once abroad and might become a rallying point. His request was refused, although it could still be granted in the future.

When the author went to see Sobukwe at his office at the University of the Witwatersrand in 1958, the P.A.C. was just emerging from the more militant youth wing of the A.N.C. Sobukwe, although his position as a lecturer in Bantu languages had led to many friendships with white members of the staff and others, emphasized in that interview that one of his principal objections to the A.N.C. was its domination by whites and Communists. Although more militant in many of his castigations of the political system, he rejected manipulation of African nationalism by people – black or white – who had a foreign ideology to promote. No official statements have been made to suggest that Sobukwe's release was contemplated because of his anti-Communist views. Indeed, the South African government's greatest strength in appeals to Western nations may be the degree to which the African nationalist movement is in Soviet-controlled hands. Therefore, the emergence abroad of a man like Sobukwe (assuming that prison life has not made deleterious personality changes) as a symbol of a non-Communist nationalist, might be the most serious blow the government could suffer in the propaganda battle of pro- and anti-South African forces in Europe and the United States.

The one leader who is in a good position to improve his own appeal is Transkeian Prime Minister Kaiser Matanzima, because he operates within the government-approved Bantustan framework. He has a celebrity value which brings school children out when he rides through Soweto streets and can make newspaper headlines both by the various pronouncements in favour of separate development and his implied criticisms of government policy. In 1961, the author drove to the home Matanzima had just built in Emigrant Tembuland to get a feel of the then promising but not yet elected politician. Today he is wont to cover up some of his feelings towards the treatment of Africans in the Republic, but in 1961 he made no bones but that Africans had had a raw deal from white people for 300 years in South Africa, and that he saw a way through separate development to make a start in redressing the balance. His support for Dr. Verwoerd was not wholly Machiavellian; Matanzima is not tongue-in-cheek in that he accepts support but hates the South African government. He genuinely sees a *modus vivendi* between black and white on the basis of equality of individual worth and separate political bases. The analogy of India and Pakistan having to break apart because of deep-seated ethnic differences, but possibly coming to a time when a formal unity will be possible, was one of the indications of future thinking Matanzima gave that day.

Despite the claim by many Afrikaner Nationalists that their policy is consistent and as unchanging – to use Dr. Verwoerd's metaphor – as a granite wall, and despite the reinforcing assertion by African nationalists (especially those abroad) that nothing changes except to get worse, Matanzima is one of the strongest evidences of a shift in thinking behind what much of the world sees as an unchanging situation. It was inconceivable a few years ago that the South African government would take over the whole floor of the leading hotel in Bloemfontein for the use of Prime Minister Matanzima and his *entourage*. There are many official examples of social cordiality between officials of the two governments. But perhaps a clue to a significant shift in attitude on the part of many Afrikaners-in-the-street was when Prime Minister Matanzima emerged from a reception at the Cape Town city hall to enter his limousine, and the Afrikaner policeman on duty snapped to attention and saluted the African politician.

Despite these changes, it is still true that the politics of African nationalism is clearly revolutionary in that it aims at a drastic re-ordering of the existing African society away from tribalism and away from the subservient role Africans play in the country. Yet violence has so far been limited by the dampening influence of the rising material living standard previously discussed. President Albert J. Luthuli of the banned African National Congress has no doubts about what he wants for his followers, but he was long inhibited by his Christianity and his conservative attitudes from going all-out for violent revolution. Younger and lesser-known leaders are outright revolutionaries. The organization and operation of an 'escape route' from the major South African cities to Botswana and further north is part of the apparatus of revolution.

It is at this stage in African nationalism that we digress to discuss Luthuli. It is worth noting that throughout the years when he was a government-paid chief doing excellent work in raising the living standards of his community, he achieved little attention outside the Republic. In his early years of political activity as head of the Natal Provincial A.N.C. and later, Luthuli preached Christian patience and non-violence.

In 1953, the author took the tarred north coast road out of Durban to see Luthuli just after his election as A.N.C. President for South Africa. The road soon wound between rounded hills carpeted with sugar cane and across dry river beds by single-lane steel bridges. There were knots of Hindu factory workers outside Gandhi Cinema – well-dressed descendants of indentured forefathers. A young Zulu un-ashamedly relieved himself by the side of the road as a car full of yell-ing European teenagers careered past. Soon after passing the site of one of Shaka's Royal Kraals, one could see smoke rising from the distant hills, the burning cane simulating another day when Shaka's *impis* raided and fired the *kraal* of a recalcitrant chief. Finally, the road crossed the Etete River, and down a winding lane that dwindled into a shady track was the small bungalow of Albert John Luthuli. It was not impressive by European standards, but the best African dwelling in the area. In front of the house a barefooted old woman (it turned out to be his aunt) was drying rice by shifting it in the sun. She greeted me in Zulu and called through the front door where I could see Luthuli struggling into a dark coat. A few minutes later, our coats were off, and we sat in chairs on the dusty stoop and leaned back in the sun of a warm autumn afternoon.

Luthuli soon made the point that Dr. Moroka's tenure as President of the A.N.C. had ended because of an intense anti-Communism which implied that all who were not with him were tainted by Communism. (When brought to court by the government over the 'Defiance' campaign, Moroka insisted on separate legal counsel from the African Communists charged with him.) A second factor in his own election, Luthuli thought, was that he has been called to Pretoria and asked to lend his weight to the government side in breaking the gathering Passive Defiance campaign. Luthuli broke with the government, lost his paid chieftainship, and stepped into the limelight.

He emphasized his pride in keeping *tsotsis* (gangsters) and their violence out of the African National Congress. He said there were Communists in the A.N.C., that we must guard against their influence. He stressed the general African attitude towards Europeans as containing an enormous amount of goodwill. Repeatedly he praised the missionaries, including American ones in his own district, and cautioned against excessive nationalism, warning that we must not some day have Africans voting for Africans without considering individual ability. Luthuli felt that the nationalism of the Afrikaners is a terrible example for African nationalism.

As the sun set across Luthuli's forty acres, he emphasized his own desire to help his people gain a better life and gave every evidence of being a strong Christian and anti-Communist. At the time one felt that the pressures were going to be very great, and the author's published conclusion at the time was that 'I couldn't help wonder whether in a tight pinch, with the government breathing down his neck, he would accept their [Communist] aid as the lesser of two evils. Maybe he is wise enough to use and not be used.'[1]

After the Passive Defiance Campaign, Luthuli still moved about South Africa and attracted large mixed, but predominately white, audiences. His success with Europeans in his 1959 speaking tour was as much an irritant to the government as his leadership of Africans.

In the later part of the 1950s, Luthuli fell under closer and closer

[1] Letter to Walter S. Rogers, Institute of Current World Affairs, New York, 6 May 1953.

government restriction. At first he was used by the Communists, who were perhaps cleverer and freer to move about, especially the white ones. He could not control the A.N.C. any longer, but he was kept as a figurehead. At some stage his tone of anti-Communism changed and he worked more openly with the South African Communist Party. In reaction against successive and successful government moves, Luthuli spoke less and less of Christian brotherhood and non-violence and finally, tacitly at first and then more openly, aligned himself with the A.N.C./Communist underground and deliberate sabotage. Luthuli did hold out for sabotage against buildings and other material objects not causing loss of life, although the saboteurs themselves soon overlooked the distinction to the point where African women and European children died.

It has been charged that the South African government deliberately restricted and hampered the non-Communist majority within the African National Congress executive so that the Communist element would gain greater power and could then be pinpointed in government propaganda at home and abroad. Such a charge is highly questionable, even though the end result is close to the facts. More likely reasons for the Communist Party influence growing within the A.N.C. are, firstly, the greater cleverness of the Communists in evading the police and, secondly, the growing frustration of the non-Communists who became willing to accept more Communist leadership.

It is exceedingly difficult to assess policy-making roles within underground organizations. However, those parts of the evidence at the Rivonia Trial which critics of the South African government do not dispute, strongly suggest that Africans as a group and non-Communists as a group were not directing the A.N.C. underground but that it had fallen to the apparently more able, possibly more dedicated, and possibly better financed Communists to make the key decisions within South Africa. Certainly, Luthuli did not know the inner secrets.

The great irony of the award by the Norwegian Parliament of the Nobel Peace Prize to Albert Luthuli was that it came a decade after he had held out a peaceful solution to South Africa's problems and had opposed the use of violence, and at a time when his name and his organization had been virtually captured by the Communists within South Africa and had turned to violent ends. It was because of the obtuse timing of the award and the seemingly cynical attitude of those who voted for it, that the award itself had little impact upon the white oligarchy in the Republic. The government argued, and not without plausibility, that the award was given primarily to embarrass the South African government and to recognize an African for the first time, not because at the time of the award Albert John Luthuli was engaged in efforts of peace and conciliation.

We have digressed to summarize the story of Luthuli because he personifies much in African nationalism as it left the early stage and went into the middle stage. Luthuli belonged to an *élite* in the sense of education, including his time at Adams College, even if that is more a high school than a college in the American sense. He was elected a chief by his small Zulu group, a fruit of democratic values; yet his being of warrior Zulu stock held an aura for many Africans at the time he became A.N.C. President. He also worked closely with Europeans – and had many European friends – without deep bitterness. He was content for many years to accept a salary from the government in Pretoria. With Luthuli, much of the seed of non-violence planted in South Africa by Mohandas Gandhi took deepest root and flowered. Luthuli was not the first in or out of the A.N.C. to struggle with Communist infiltration and direction. But the Communist thrust was more powerful and the restrictions placed upon him by the government made him weaker in combating it than some predecessors. He tried to make common cause, but in the end had been more used than obeyed. Although he stretched his heart and even his principles to understand and accommodate the feelings of the younger Africans, he could not keep the more militant ones with him. The restrictions placed on him by the government and his own failing health suggest that although alive and still receiving occasional visitors as this book is written, he has moved into history as one of the most significant leaders of his people into the intermediate stage of African nationalism. Possibly a dramatic escape from South Africa, a course urged on him from some quarters, would give him a new role, but not within South Africa.

INTERMEDIATE AND PRESENT STAGE

In the intermediate stage of nationalism, we find African nationalism has certainly matured in some respects, but is only beginning in most. Loyalty values have not shifted downwards, but are held most intensely by the better-educated and more prosperous African upper-middle and upper class. This continued restriction of attitude accounts in part for the relative lack of violence. While it may be said that Africans as a whole have little to lose and much to gain from violent revolution, it is also true that African leadership has a great deal to lose. Succeeding generations of upper-middle-class Africans have built a material stake in their community that is risked with reluctance. A driving, devil-may-care sense of dedication was more evident in the youth, and accounted for the greater militancy in 1960 of the Pan Africanist Congress. Nationalist slogans and symbols spread through the African schools and in various communications media until the government suppressed them. After the Sharpeville shootings in 1960, Bantu announcers on the government-controlled radio network played patriotic African songs with revolutionary slogans in the vernaculars; much later, when this was discovered, the Bantu announcers were fired.

Trade union activities have been gaining ground, although technically African unions are not recognized under the Industrial Conciliation Act, and are illegal. European employers have pressed for legislation of African unions to allow for at least a hypothetically non-political outlet for workers' grievances.

Despite the low economic positions of Africans, the patterns of their economic power have become quite complex. When an African gasoline or petrol-station owner can show a yearly profit of over the equivalent of $60,000 and a number of Africans own a string of businesses or several farms, economic complexities have developed. But African rural advance has been retarded because of the general practice of communal ownership of land in the tribal reserves, overcrowding, and the system of migrant labour which removes many of the most productive people for the productive years of their lives, even though their cash income is at present vital to their families in the reserve.

The sense of dedication of many people in politics tends to lack continuity and is related to the effect of charisma. While there is a decline in the 'messiah' concept among Africans, the continual harassing by the police and restrictive legislation make the building of a solid organization difficult. Thus an individual who can put together a number of supporters rapidly will soon leap into prominence. But there is neither a single leader nor a group of leaders with whom interested outsiders, including the South African government, could deal directly. Left alone, it is likely that African nationalism in the Republic would soon develop its own distinct pattern and lose its dependence upon foreign example. But under conditions inside the country, there remains a dependence upon foreign ideas, as indeed a lessened one on foreign capital. Nevertheless, it can be said that African nationalists in the Republic are not waiting for foreign allies to do all the work for them. Those who contact other African nationalists outside South Africa usually return home with renewed faith in the quality of their own leadership. It is but another aspect of the growing anomaly that in all of sub-Sahara Africa, the greatest depth of potential African leadership is in South Africa.

It is also striking that this leadership cannot be identified in the Republic today. We discussed the 'names' such as Luthuli, Mandela, and Sobukwe in concluding our examination of the early stage of African nationalism. They have no replacements and will not have them within the present political pattern. African politics are so complex and so involved with so many able people inside the Republic that it is extremely unlikely that any of the numerous exiled leaders will emerge as a symbol to Africans within the Republic. There are those who carry on titles they had in South Africa. But they also carry on many of the differences and feuds which were at least minor divisive forces at home. The deepest struggle for over forty years in the African nationalism of the Republic has been between the predominately non-Communist African leadership and the Communists, both black and white.

This underlay the great schism giving rise to the P.A.C., with its reputed 'black nationalism' and greater militancy, culminating in the immediately sensational and world attention-getting Sharpeville affair.

One of the parallels between Afrikaner and African nationalism is in their claim to be rooted in the soil of Africa. It is not inappropriate to hark back to English–Afrikaner differences and interject the following quotation: 'Afrikaner nationalism is a dynamic force, because it is not a foreign importation. It has its roots deep down in the heart of every Afrikaner. It is an insuppressible urge towards self-realization, self-determination, independence and freedom.'

The above quotation has been altered from its true form only by substituting 'Afrikaner' where it should read 'African'. It comes from the 1949 Declaration of the African National Congress Youth League. Furthermore, the Pan Africanists claim that this viewpoint is part of the main platform of those who broke away from the African National Congress in 1958.

Today, the A.N.C. in exile denounces its earlier statement as racialistic and the inverse of Afrikaner Nationalism. What lies behind the contemporary A.N.C. attack is the exclusiveness of the P.A.C., which has virtually excluded whites and thus, today, questions the acceptability within African nationalism of white Communists. The P.A.C. rejects the class approach of Marxist ideology for Sobukwe has long claimed that Africans are one as a class and that only they are genuinely interested in drastic change.

Whether its approach was 'black racialism' or not, the Pan Africanists were remarkably successful in appealing to African emotions against the more intellectual pull of the A.N.C. in the period preceding Sharpeville, and probably up until the final banning of the two groups. The appeal of the Matanzimas has been called 'black racialism' or 'black pride' or 'opportunism', but it has similar roots to that of the P.A.C., although the plant above the ground may bear different fruit. What no movement has touched is African labour on white farms. Some three million in number, some of them little more than sharecroppers, they have lain outside urban nationalism and rural tribalism. Shortly before his arrest, Sobukwe was beginning to organize these Africans.

To return to the Sharpeville watershed, the shouting and rock-throwing P.A.C. march of some hundreds of supporters until they were almost ringing and pressing on the police station did cause the handful of young white policemen, scared and conscious of the fate a few days before of white and black police torn to pieces by an angry crowd in Natal, to open fire without orders. The slaughter was instant. Even though the police fired for only a few seconds, most of the mob immediately turned to flee and were shot from behind. They were truly

shots heard round the world. World opinion crystallized as never before against South Africa and the country itself was in chaos for days.
The unfortunate police officer, who had never given the order to fire
and courageously leapt in front of them to stop it, was shortly there-
after retired, a different and unhappy person.

But the aftermath of Sharpeville, including the widespread arrests by
the police, left the Pan Africanist Congress a broken force. The P.A.C.
did evolve internally into a terroristic group known simply as 'Poqo',
which was successful in murdering a number of Africans and Europeans. As Judge President Beyers of the Cape Supreme Court sentenced
a group of P.A.C./Poqo members who had set out with sharp *pangas*
to take over Cape Town, he commented on their foolhardiness and
over-estimation of their chances, while genuinely attempting to understand their deeper frustrations and aspirations. In seeking material on
the P.A.C. in 1962, the author interviewed the then head of the organization, Potlako Leballo, in his exile headquarters in Lesotho. Rarely if
ever, in twenty years' experience with African nationalism in all of the
countries south of the Sahara, had one been asked to swallow such pre-
posterous dreams and such sweeping lies as Leballo insisted upon. The
absolute certainty with which he said, 'I will see you in Pretoria in 1963
because I will let you come into our country', was characteristic of the
sense of unwarranted optimism and megalomania which eventually
contributed to a rejection of him as P.A.C. head by many of his
followers.

The deep split between the A.N.C. and the P.A.C. over the issue of
ideology and of tactics, only roughly correlating with experience versus
age, has been followed by the fracturing of both organizations. This is
not the book to delineate all of the splinterings which have taken place
outside the country. The last elected President of the A.N.C.,
Oliver Tambo, is still felt by most close observers (including South
African government sources) to be outside the Communist Party.
Tambo is still forced to work under an umbrella which includes not only
old Communist Party hacks, both white and black, but new recruits
whose allegiance is sometimes doubted by both sides. The desperate
need for finance has led to many accusations of who is providing it,
not only within party ranks, but among the various headquarters of the
A.N.C. in London, Dar es Salaam, and elsewhere.

The Pan Africanist Congress is even more shattered. Its one prominent white leader, Patrick Duncan, the son of the first South African-
born Governor-General of South Africa, was first pushed out to
Algiers from the London office, and later involved in further disagree-
ments. The five sections of the P.A.C. at the present writing in 1966
will most probably have re-formed into other groups by the time these
words are read. What is significant is that one of these wings has devia-
ted so far from the original premise of the P.A.C. that it has accepted
financial assistance from Peking.

The politics of exile could fill many pages and include some significantly different angles if the South West Africa groups were included.
But what is germane is that these exiled nationalist individuals exercise
an influence as pressure groups upon African states, in Britain, in
Europe, and also in the United States, to a far greater extent than they
influence events within South Africa itself.

After the breakup of the mass African movements and the arrest or
escape abroad of most of the top echelons of the white Communist
organizations, there was one last effort of that 'generation' of militantly
anti-government Africans, Indians, and whites to strike effectively. It
was Operation Mayibuye. Based on a secluded farm conveniently
located between Johannesburg and Pretoria, but with property called
'Travallyn' near Krugersdorp for the manufacture of guerilla weapons,
and a hideout in the southern suburbs of Johannesburg, it was expected
by its planners to become the spark for a general conflagration. Most
of the eight defendants convicted (one man was acquitted and two
escaped) in the so-called 'Rivonia Trial' freely admitted their plans to
engineer acts of violence and destruction throughout South Africa.
They were charged under the Sabotage Act and not for High Treason,
which requires stricter proof.

Although before the trial the South African Communist Party
circulated a pamphlet predicting the trial would be a 'frame-up', an
attitude which found reflection in some foreign papers, the actual
defence was not that sabotage was not planned and would not have
been carried out but, rather, that conditions of African life in South
Africa are so unjust and oppressive as to justify such acts against the
state. This frank attitude, most forcefully expressed by Nelson Mandela
and later put forward with great candour by Advocate Abram Fischer

(who defended at the Rivonia Trial) when he was himself on trial in 1966, along with the massive evidence found by the police when they broke in and caught most of the defendants red-handed with incriminating documents, has put an end to the period in which the Communist Party in South Africa hid behind various liberal fronts and in which intimations of its linkage with the African National Congress could be waved off as unproven McCarthy-like charges.

If the whole Operation Mayibuye (Operation 'Come-Back') had succeeded in 1963, it would have marked a rapid but final phase of the whole African nationalist movement, at least as conceived by a small but well-organized interracial team. Prime Minister Verwoerd stated in Parliament, with the support of the white opposition, that all racial groups would have lost their freedom. Those who plotted revolution obviously disagreed – at least in so far as the non-white groups are concerned. What the broad mass of Africans felt or thought is not ascertainable. Certainly, there would have been differences of opinion. Within the broad white community, the mass of information concerning armed revolt which came out of the Rivonia Trial did have a profound effect. The view of hundreds of thousands of whites who disliked many aspects of government racial policy is best summed up by an editorial on the trial in the *Rand Daily Mail*, the most vigorous critic of the government among the daily press. On 17 June 1966, the editor wrote:

> The sentences pronounced by Mr. Justice De Wet in Pretoria yesterday at the conclusion of the Rivonia Trial were both wise and just. The law is at its best when there is firmness tinged with mercy, and this was the case yesterday. The sentences could not have been less severe than those passed. The men found guilty had organized sabotage on a wide scale, and had plotted armed revolution. As the Judge pointed out, the crime of which they were found guilty was essentially high treason. The death penalty would have been justified.

But while Rivonia ended a chapter in the book of African nationalism in South Africa, it did not end the story. The *Rand Daily Mail* has gone on to champion the African cause against what the *Mail* and many whites, as well as most Africans in South Africa, feel is an unjust situation.

With the old methods of establishing a power base denied to African

I

nationalists as such, the stage within South Africa is being taken over, as planned by key figures within the Afrikaners' National Party, by essentially tribally based Africans. The Matanzimas, as well as the various successors to the Victor Potos, of the Transkei have their counterparts in other tribal areas. This infant nationalism is not really African nationalism in the sense of the last three decades. Chief Victor Poto has protested to the writer that the opposition in the Transkei favours a South African nationalism regardless of race, and is only in a broad and non-antagonistic sense an African nationalism. Still Poto's route to power, as he was seeking to follow it, was through his appeal to the Xhosa people of the Transkei. What is developing in the rural areas is a Xhosa, Zulu and a Sotho nationalism. This trend is encouraged by the nature of the uni-tribal states, the British-named Basutoland, Swaziland, and Bechuanaland. Their independence, achieved or forthcoming, has been gained by or given to what are essentially 'nations' built upon tribes. The political genius of Moshesh in the middle of the nineteenth century was to create out of the shattered remnants of beaten tribes a sense of what the Basuto – from mountain shepherd to urban attorney – refer to as the 'Basuto Nation'. The new names – Lesotho, Botswana, and Swazi – are themselves symbols of what is at base modernized tribalism.

Without digressing far from our theme, it is highly significant that in Swaziland the British government has felt it necessary to prepare compensation – the 'golden handshake' in decolonialization jargon – for Zulu as well as English civil servants. Comparably, the feeling in Umtata of the 'Transkei for the Transkeians' may be a throwback to a cruder nationalism, but it is none the less a fact.

None of the foregoing thesis regarding the tribally based nationalisms implies a judgement that because the path being followed is one encouraged directly by the National Party or indirectly by Her Majesty's governments, both Conservative and Labour, they will necessarily succeed. It is likely that far from assuaging the sense of discrimination felt by most Bantu people of southern Africa, these new nationalisms will be the base from which to press for greater rights and opportunities.

It is no coincidence that there is co-operation between Matanzima's Transkeian government and the South African government, and that it depends on the South African government for 80 per cent of its budget. However, the proud, firm, but friendly hand extended by Lesotho Prime Minister Leabua Jonathan to South Africa is not a result of military power. Helpless as Lesotho is militarily, South Africa would risk more militarily by attacking it than could possibly be gained. Some official political support was rendered to Jonathan in arrangements for electioneering on the Witwatersrand favouring the Basutoland National Party. Far more important is the economic pressure which exists for Lesotho as it does to a lesser extent with Botswana and Swaziland. But these three territories and the Transkei do have a new tribe-nation in common, and they do have a cautious *modus vivendi* with white South Africa as part of their individual 'foreign' policies.

In such an industrial country as South Africa, it is not likely that political leadership will be held in the long run as the primary preserve of rural areas. Political expression in the huge city of Soweto is kept down by legislation enforced by the police and muted by the rising standard of living. A prominent American Negro banker, highly respected for his business acumen and strong hand in civil rights in the United States, toured South Africa in both 1961 and 1965. He was deeply impressed by the relatively affluent African society, especially in the cities such as Soweto, where he noted a sharp increase of homes with garages and larger and more expensive cars. But he was also critical of much sharper government restrictions on Africans who wished to add to their flourishing garage, dry-cleaning, and other commercial enterprises.

Some of the political drive of the more prosperous Africans of the Republic may be siphoned off through the Bantustans. But the Bantustans are not likely ever to provide an adequate answer by themselves. Concomitant and imaginative steps are needed in urban areas of the Republic. People want to have a say as to where they work, where their children go to school, and about the parks they play in. There is a revival of African local government in the townships of South Africa, and some of the Africans on boards are gaining a measure of political leadership. There does remain a vacuum between these virtually advisory posts, plus the economically strong African businessman of the cities on the one hand and the new tribally based nationalism in the rural areas on the other.

African nationalism in the Republic has thus been thwarted as it moved from the early to the middle stage in a way that applied rarely to the Afrikaners, such as the 1877–80 Passive Resistance Movement in the Transvaal, when M. W. Pretorious Bok and others were imprisoned. But where there are grievances, there will be protests, no matter how suppressed or delayed, until they are met or sublimated. Barring outside intervention, African nationalism in the Republic has mutated into a path of lesser resistance, if not possibly greater final success.

CHAPTER VIII

RELATIONSHIPS WITH CONTINENTAL AND WORLD POWERS

T he relationships of Afrikaner and African nationalisms with other forces on the African continent as well as in the world at large are much narrower in focus than the relationships of South Africa in general.

The mimetic impulses of African nationalism within the Republic are prevented from finding significant models to follow elsewhere on the continent. Encouragement to strive for rights, pride in seeing African ambassadors in the United Nations, and a very scanty knowledge of the cultural tradition of West Africa, for example, have a limited political impact. When some South African Bantu leaders dream and plan of controlling the affairs of the Republic, some of them see it as the most powerful state on the African continent which would teach and help, not learn from or be aided by, poorer states to the north.

Nationalism in the former High Commission Territories offers more immediate ideas as to what courses African nationalism in the Republic will follow. One of the influences on their nationalism is to make Africans in the Republic more tribally conscious. While this is immediately denied by some sophisticated Africans, it is a fact that a southern Africa in which Bechuanas think of themselves as citizens of Botswana, Swazis of Swaziland, and Basutos of Lesotho, conceptualizes the tribal type of nationalism to Xhosa-speaking and other Republican people. Indeed, experience in Swaziland suggests that a sense of nation growing out of tribalism may well be a pattern for the Republic.

Up until a few months before the 1963 elections in Swaziland, Her Majesty's government acted as though King Sobhuza was an anachronistic holdover, the Swazi 'nation' a hollow memory of a few old illiterates, and that modern and progressive political parties would occupy the centre of the political stage. The overwhelming success of the neither modern nor progressive Imbokodvo Party, initially in co-operation with conservative white businessmen, was followed by a rush of educated and progressive Swazis to climb aboard the bandwagon and to provide additional leadership so that they could come out of a political wilderness. The need of the 'Swazi Nation' for an infusion of 'progressive Swazi' laid the basis of a broadening and further unifica-tion of almost all Swazi after 1965.

The idea that African nationalism in the Republic might go through a broad stage of greater tribal roots is anathema to the exile leadership, but not necessarily to local African leaders still within the Republic. The theory of an all-conquering nationalism without a basis in race or tribe has many practical hurdles to climb among Africans as well as among the whites of the Republic. Swaziland is a microcosm of some Republican issues. As suggested, the attitudes of the Swazi majority towards government employment passed very swiftly from (1) localization with equal opportunity for everyone resident in or at least born in Swaziland, regardless of race, to (2) Africanization or equal opportunity for all Africans, to (3) Swazization or equal opportunity for all Swazis. Thus, as early as 1965, the Queen's Commissioner had to begin thinking of compensation not just for Europeans being re-placed, but for Zulus who held many of the key posts in education and the police.

Because Bechuanaland and Basutoland had fewer 'alien' Africans, the problem was nothing like the same. However, tribally based national-ism in each of the three territories was such that good relations with the Republic of South Africa were genuinely desired. This led to bitter resentment of Africans from the Republic who accepted the freely offered political asylum but attempted to use the territories as sanctua-ries from which to launch sabotage against the Republic. The strong traditional and conservative element in tribal nationalism finds an accommodation with the conservative South African government, de-spite racial differences. They appear to recognize, as Lesotho Prime Minister Leabua Jonathan wrote to the author, the 'uniqueness of our problems and the need for unique methods for their solution'.[1]

[1] December 1965.

The three territories have a great significance to Afrikaner nationalism. Among the many Afrikaner nationalist views of the general concept of Bantustans (including idealism, self-deception, or outright deceit), those who hold a goal of genuine independence depend heavily upon Lesotho, Botswana, and Swaziland.

Those Afrikaners who have a sincere approach to 'Bantustans' – and this may or may not comprise a majority of the leadership at a given time – have for the most part arrived at their views from an analysis of Afrikaner nationalism. The argument is in essence simple. If we as Afrikaners so value our freedom and our right to organize our own 'nation' that we have fought and will fight for it, then we will never be truly safe until there is a concomitant outlet for the aspirations of Africans. Most Afrikaner nationalist leaders who have given thought to this would prefer to think of Zulu nationalism and Tswana nationalism rather than 'African' nationalism, but all agree that the safety of Afrikaner nationalism requires an outlet – some way of African nationalism reaching the final stage of maturation without at the same time destroying what Afrikaners value.

The Transkei was the first effort towards such an outlet. It has been more successful than its critics forecast, although it has fallen far short of providing the full and final control of their destiny to the Xhosa people – either the 2,000,000 in the Transkei or the 1,500,000 Xhosa being born, working, and dying in 'European' South Africa. How the Bantustan policy may evolve (for certainly it will not be static) – whether towards more Bantustans with greater autonomy, some form of partition, or abandonment to pure *baasskap* – is not the point here.

What is significant is that many of those Afrikaners who see the salvation of their nationalism in accommodating Xhosa or African nationalism, are also acutely aware of the shortage of time to demonstrate to Africans within the Republic as well as to a hostile world that a *modus vivendi* lies somewhere along these lines. To these Afrikaners the British 'Southern African territories' are tremendously important. For if Afrikaner nationalism can come to terms with Basuto nationalism, then it may in time come to terms with Zulu nationalism. If South Africa can prove itself a friendly neighbour and not a menacing giant to the Bechuana, the government of the Republic may gain itself time. Furthermore, the enormous accumulation of sheer racial prejudice which results when you lump together the views of all whites in the Republic may well be softened more rapidly through the example of racial tolerance and ability of African governments in the three territories than by all the preaching or finger-pointing of the world at large.

The Transkei and any other 'homeland' must be so financially dependent upon the Republic for years to come as to cast valid doubts as to its freedom to follow an independent political course. But despite the economic pressures upon them to be friendly with the Republic, the African governments of the neighbouring territories do have the alternative of not co-operating and of being bases for attack. Small and weak as they are, the territories have great political strength with Great Britain behind them and the rest of the world watching with partisan eyes. The question of 'internal interference in the affairs of a neighbouring country' which the white Rhodesians criticize Britain for, is also South Africa's argument against U.N. interference in South Africa. However, if South Africa 'took over' one of the defenceless territories, the finger of shame would not then be pointed by South Africa but towards South Africa. It is well recognized in the Union Buildings in Pretoria, where the South African Cabinet meets, that the *bona fides* of Afrikaner theoretical treatment of the nationalism of Africans in the Republic through the Bantustan approach, will be judged by the interplay of Afrikaner nationalism with the nationalism of the Basuto, Swazi, and Bechuana. Time will judge the depth of sincerity and Afrikaner support for Dr. Verwoerd's declaration in the March 1966 election campaign that: 'We are nationalists. We understand the desire of nations to be just themselves and themselves alone. We can understand the deep feeling arising in black and white and are prepared to live with it.'

Afrikaners are not the only whites in southern Africa to face the problem of nationalism. The Portuguese yield to no nation in the intensity of official feelings. They too have both a white and a black nationalism problem which may well have an accelerating impact upon the binary South African nationalism. This is particularly true as closer ties have developed in the 1960s between South Africa and the Portuguese territories, such as co-operative development along the Cunene in South West Africa, a development bank, greater South African investment in Mozambique, and the markedly increased travel which preceded but has also been heightened by the new air routings through Angola and to Portugal itself. Events in Angola and Mozambique are closer to South Africa than they have ever been in the previous three centuries. Economic co-operation, particularly in regard to oil supplies from Luanda in the event of a boycott, could grow rapidly.

The 'white' nationalism of Angola and Mozambique is in abeyance and internal or external African forces threaten the stability of the régime. But when these die down, the feelings of a substantial percentage of the permanent non-African population in both territories for greater autonomy, if not independence, rise to the surface. The Portuguese government has taken cognizance of this in meeting demands for local universities and more local decision-making.

It is anomalous that the European nation most sympathetic to racial intermarriage in its African territory – for French fraternity at a high and official level was not translated to intermarriage at the *petit bourgeois* level to the extent of the Portuguese – should find itself the strongest neighbour of the country with a government most dedicated to racial separation. In practice, of course, there has been considerable mixing in past decades in South Africa, and considerable racial prejudice in both Angola and Mozambique, but the theoretical views are poles apart. Christianity in Africa knows no greater cleavage of the major denominations than the Catholicism of the Portuguese and the Calvinism of the Dutch Reform Churches. The long and nearly absolute rule of Salazar also contrasts with the frequent elections within the white oligarchy of South Africa and a much greater responsiveness to the wishes of the electorate.

Given such philosophical, social, and political opposites, it is not surprising that Afrikaner and Portuguese nationalisms have failed to significantly influence each other. Mutual economic interest allowed regulation of the movement of mine labourers and of freight, but even here the philosophical interests clashed. In 1953, the then-Governor Gabriel Teixera of Mozambique told the author that, 'Here in Lourenço Marques our biggest problem with the natives is the dislike and distrust they acquire when working in South Africa. I have no more human rights than any Native in Mozambique. We are all human beings with our own personal dignity.' The former admiral said the key word summing up the difference between Portuguese and South African policy was *dignidad* (dignity).

Much water has flowed down the Cunene since then, and the self-interests of Afrikaners and Portuguese have thrown them closer together. The Afrikaner people generally have become less suspicious of Catholicism and the Portuguese less suspicious of outside financial investments from friendly countries. Both are sufficiently pragmatic not to let philosophical differences erect an absolute barrier to a common market of southern Africa. However, a significant interaction of the white nationalisms is not to be expected barring extreme circumstances.

The Portuguese contacts of both of South Africa's nationalisms – white and black – are limited by language barriers. Very few white South Africans speak Portuguese; only a handful of Portuguese speak Afrikaans. The language of 'white' communication is English, a language spoken by only a minority of Portuguese, both officials and residents, in Angola and Mozambique. Lourenço Marques businessmen are likely to know English but the contact is still limited. The flow of ideas is sharply limited by the inability of Afrikaners and Portuguese to read a common language.

African contacts are even more severely limited by language. Those few Africans in Angola and Mozambique who are literate use Portuguese. There is the natural communication of members of tribes on two sides of the border, notably the Ovambo in South West Africa and the Shangaans in southern Mozambique, but neither language carries very far inside any of the countries. The most likely basis for contact between an African nationalist in South Africa and a Bakongo from the war zone of northern Angola is that American missionaries may have passed on some English to the Angolan. Between Mozambique Africans and the Republican Africans, a rudimentary verbal communication is possible in Fanagalo, the language of the mines based upon Zulu. In Dar es Salaam, relations between the 'Freedom Fighters' of Frelimo and the 'Freedom Fighters' from South Africa have not proved to be particularly congenial.

Although their countries have common boundaries, the African nationalists in South Africa, Angola, and Mozambique have not – like the whites – influenced each other significantly. Eduardo Mondlane,

Frelimo leader from southern Mozambique, began his undergraduate education at Witwatersrand, where he was strongly influenced by liberal ideas of the English-speaking white students, but his case is atypical.

In addition to the language barrier, another factor has been the highly restricted activity of 'left' political organization in the Portuguese territories and, in particular, the lack of a Communist Party. The predominately white Communist influence from time to time within the African National Congress – the most sophisticated and internationally oriented group of Nationalists – did not have anything like the major ties with neighbouring Portuguese territories that they had with London or Moscow. Although transportation between the Witwatersrand and Mozambique was quite easy by car, train, or plane until recent years, and is still feasible, travel from South Africa to Angola is practical only by air, with a high cost factor and easy identification of travellers.

In the realm of white politics the principal relationship of nationalisms has been between Rhodesia and the Republic; the days of white political groupings in Zambia and Malawi never developed very far and are largely a memory. The accession to power of African governments in the two northern territories of the Federation strengthened the determination of some Afrikaners in the Republic to succeed in the National Party's policies, but only as a reflection of the general tide of African nationalism on the continent.

Throughout most of its history, white Rhodesian politics have contained a reaction against and not an influence from the white politics of the Republic. The refusal to become a province of the Union in 1922 was an early manifestation of this. If, in effect, another 'English' Natal had been added to the Union, the course of South African politics might have been spectacularly different. But in the four decades following the refusal of General Smuts's proposal of incorporation, there was little sentiment on either side of the Limpopo for union. While the South African Party rule, and later that of the United Party in the Republic, has many parallels with the way the white establishment ruled then Southern Rhodesia, the force of Afrikaner nationalism was not involved except as a whipping-boy in Rhodesian politics. Afrikaners in Rhodesia, concentrated in the deep south, were usually supporters of the whole succession of loosely knit and politically inept opposition groups.

Under the pressure of African nationalism in the 1950s, white political leadership in the two countries moved in opposite directions. South Africa tightened up its laws involving white and black, while Rhodesia, which in many ways had been much stricter than South Africa, loosened them in liberal ways and at a pace which has never been duplicated by any white government on the continent. The subsequent and successive shifts to the right of the Rhodesia government as measured through Prime Ministers from Todd to Whitehead to Field to Smith, would superficially appear to bring the two countries together. Indeed, by the time of the Unilateral Declaration of Independence, it could be fairly argued that the Rhodesian government was well to the right of the South African.

None of this made a real impact upon Afrikaner nationalism. Rhodesia attracted a substantial number of more liberally minded English-speaking people from South Africa, including some highly useful for government posts, but with the collapse of the 'liberal boom' in Rhodesia after Whitehead's party was defeated, there was a reverse flow to the Republic. Afrikaner nationalism had been fighting too long against 'English' concepts in southern Africa to be much affected by the import of liberal ideas. Yet paradoxically, when Rhodesia passed into the U.D.I. phase, the thinkers inside Afrikaner nationalism were critical of the Smith régime for not providing sufficient outlet (at least in its theory or lack of theory) for the force of African nationalism. The point at which the two white political groupings had the most in common was when Welensky and Verwoerd could agree during their repeated meetings in Pretoria and at the Cape. They didn't see eye-to-eye in their policies – quite different from each other on paper – but they appeared to recognize that the other man had a policy which to him seemed to have a certain consistency and chance of success. But it would be wrong to imply that just because Verwoerd opposed Ian Smith's *baasskap* in principle, he thought eventual majority rule under the Welensky formula was a wise solution.

Although the Rhodesian Front under Smith appeared to many Afrikaners to be similar to the National Party – and indeed the Argus Press chain of papers in Rhodesia and South Africa were finally alike in their criticisms of the two governments – the *rapport* was not the same. Several politically far-right supporters of the National Party such as Ivor Benson moved from Pretoria to Salisbury and played a role in the Front, but this was after the influence of some of these men had waned within the National Party. Afrikaner nationalism is *sui generis* in South Africa and influenced far more from within than from without.

This is certainly not the case for African nationalism in Rhodesia. Joshua Nkomo and other Rhodesian Africans were educated in South Africa and followed closely political developments within the Republic. One could analyse in considerable detail the impact of African national-ism in the Republic upon Rhodesia, but the reverse influence has been limited. With the detention of both Z.A.P.U. (Zimbabwe African Peoples Union) and Z.A.N.U. (Zimbabwe African National Union) leaders within Rhodesia, the shift of nationalist headquarters to Dar es Salaam further removed black Rhodesian nationalism from a direct influence upon the Republic.

Malawi and Zambia have not been important in South Africa's politics, but they do hold some potential. Dr. Banda's predilection for blunt speaking notwithstanding, he has said that many of the problems of southern Africa are solvable in a realistic context. His outright sympathy for the position taken by Lesotho's National Party was re-flected in Banda's comment to an emissary of Chief Johnathan: 'I know the problems of South Africa and of your relations and I agree with your position.' The odds are certainly against it, but if the South African government were ever to exchange diplomatic relations with a state north of the Zambezi, Malawi is the most likely candidate.

Zambian Prime Minister Kenneth Kaunda has numerous admirers in South Africa among both Europeans and Africans. Soon after he came to power behind the scenes in Pretoria there were high hopes of friendly ties. The major role as a copper producer in Zambia of the Anglo-American Corporation (neither Anglo nor American, but South African) and the goodwill in Zambia towards Anglo Chairman Harry Oppenheimer were mentioned as possible links. Oppenheimer denied that his personally good relations with Kaunda had any relation to the South African government. Observers also noted that one of the largest American investors in South Africa, Charles Engelhard (who maintains a home and diverse interests there), was picked to head the United States delegation for Zambian independence.

However, the kidnapping in Zambia of a European wanted by the South African police and his subsequent discovery alive on the shores of Zoo Lake in Johannesburg led to recriminations. The improvement of a landing strip in South West Africa's Caprivi Strip bordering Zambia led to Zambian charges that an offensive air force base was being built by South Africa, although the contracting was being done by Rhodesian and Zambian firms. In spite of some observers' high hopes, it seems unlikely that Prime Minister Kaunda will have a role as a so-called 'moderate' in the South African situation. When he laid down conditions in the popular press for closer relations with South Africa, the highly formal South African Foreign Office backed well away. African militants in the Republic do not feel the need for a 'moderate' to talk, but for a revolutionary to act with the backing of far more power than Zambia can muster.

Other African states do have an impact upon African nationalist organizations with offices in the African countries. But despite the Liberation Committee of the Organization of African States and frequent condemnations of South Africa in the United Nations the individual African states make almost no direct impact upon either Afrikaner or African nationalism. Listening to debates in the United Nations or sitting before a continental map in groups considering national policy, one is lulled into seeing Africa as shrinking in size and taking on a one-ness it does not have in actuality. In Accra or Nairobi or Tananarive or Casablanca, one feels physically farther from South Africa than in New York or London. On the continent, the vastness of distances and difficulties of communication, let alone the problem of transporting the ultimate political force of military power, all seem to place South Africa very far away.

This is reflected in the thoughtful analysis of *The Foreign Policy of African States* by Doudou Thiam,[1] the Foreign Minister of Senegal. In his discussion of the ideology of nationalism and socialism, of relations between the African states, of their relations with foreign powers, and of future African unity, M. Thiam mentions South Africa only three times in his book, always in passing as an exception to the other inde-

[1] London, Phoenix, 1965.

pendent states. South Africa's usefulness as a rallying point of Pan African unity has perhaps diminished in recent years as the continent appears to have turned inward to solving what are more national or domestic problems. When South Africa is at issue, the negative unity does not produce a sophisticated study of ideology within the Republic or of what the future might bring except the Republic's stark 'defeat'.

Afrikaner and African nationalisms are opposites when it comes to influence outside Africa. The Afrikaners are less and less influenced by what outsiders *think* even though they take cognizance of what outsiders *do* or might do. African nationalists are more intermeshed with outside thinking than ever before.

We have traced the mimetic period when Afrikaners were at first fascinated with National Socialism and then sought to loose themselves from its grip. Today, the greatest bitterness is exhibited towards the Netherlands, the United States, and Great Britain. For a long time, leading Afrikaners have known that any romantic concept of Holland as 'mother country' and therefore sympathetic, was unrealistic. It has been a bitter pill for many Dutch-born and Dutch-educated Afrikaners to swallow. But this was not true of Dutch-born Dr. Verwoerd, who had not shown particular regard for Holland. The rending of close theological ties has been even more painful. The peculiar sense of hurt Afrikaners felt in 1965 when the Dutch government contributed to the Defence and Aid Fund was compared, by a Dutchman naturalized as a South African, with his own hurt when the Nazi bombing of Rotterdam elicited so little sympathy among the Afrikaners a generation ago. This is not the place to describe Afrikaner–Dutch relations, but even within the Republic they have traditionally been stiff rather than cordial. The epithet *kaaskop* ('cheesehead') that the Afrikaners hurl at the Dutchman has more sting now than ever. Ideologically there are no nationalist links to Holland.

Afrikaner nationalism thinks of itself as anti-colonial, democratic, Christian, and a defender against Communism. The Americans wave a similar flag. But not until 1965, although indications to the contrary were noted much earlier, did the leaders of Afrikaner nationalism really begin to realize that whatever their concept of being part of 'the West', the American government, in the State Department in particular, had another interpretation. No doubt the omnipotent military power of the U.S. *vis-à-vis* South Africa intensified the backlash of anger against the Americans which swept through the National Party in 1964–6.

The intense anti-Americanism of higher levels of the National Party stems from a variety of incidents, most of them unpublicized, and from certain assumptions about American society. A continual irritation from the Afrikaner viewpoint was the somewhat stagey 'mixed parties' held by American missions on the Fourth of July and other U.S. holidays. This persisted, whereas the American switch from trying to defeat Tshombe in battle to acceptance and support of him became less an issue. A *contretemps* over what should have been a routine request for the aircraft carrier *Independence* to dock in Cape Town, escalated to Prime Minister Verwoerd's desk and a major incident. Speaking at a political rally in the northern Cape, Dr. Verwoerd lashed back at the Americans, saying that American Negroes would not be allowed to man a 'deep space' tracking station near Pretoria. The station has been exceptionally well run by the South Africans themselves and the chances of the one or two liaison men being an American Negro scientist were extremely slight, but the American government reluctantly took cognizance of the statement and reaffirmed that it would not discriminate on the grounds of colour. Although the United States urgently needs the deep space facility, because a new station in Spain and one on an Atlantic island only partly duplicate it, the future of the Pretoria station is threatened by both South African and American attitudes. A political confidant of the Prime Minister's later described the tracking station comment as one of the very few political errors Dr. Verwoerd had made.

On the other side, senior American diplomats in Johannesburg engaged in activities with members of the African community which would certainly be highly suspect in the U.S. if a foreign embassy had similar relations with an anti-Viet Nam group of Americans. Experienced American businessmen in Johannesburg resented pressure from an American official to make them advertise in a new Coloured publication. Perhaps most of the provocations have been accidental. It is sheer misunderstanding sometimes, as when the now Commanding General of the South African Army, General Rudolph C. Hiemstra, was refused an entry visa to visit the U.S., when the Americans were merely trying to delay his visit until after a critical period at the United Nations. Not long afterwards the head of the South African security system was able to travel incognito to Washington. G. Mennen Williams, as Assistant Secretary of State for Africa, irritated the South Africans most at the beginning of his term of office in 1961, when he spoke of 'Africa for the Africans', and at the end in 1966 when he implied that the U.S. would bring down South Africa by sanctions except that they would not work. The hearings in the Congress, on activities of U.S. business concerns in South Africa, conducted by Representative Barrett O'Hara, provided another source of annoyance to South Africans in 1966.

The list of incidents exacerbating relations between the United States and South Africa could be much expanded. The significance of all of them is that the one-time feeling of a certain togetherness on the international scene, as when South African planes flew side by side with the Americans in the Korean War, has changed radically in a decade. Afrikaner nationalists are resentful of what many of them view as deliberate distortions and unfair political comment in much of the U.S. reporting on the Republic. There is suspicion that the American Field Service exchange programme of high school-age South Africans and Americans is an attempt to indoctrinate the South Africans. A similar suspicion exists in concerned American circles that the South African Foundation invites key Europeans and Americans to the Republic for the sole purpose of a one-sided indoctrination. And the United States–South African Leader Exchange Programme, which has exchanged over two hundred leaders of all races in both countries, has been violently denounced from both the South African right and anti-South African organizations in America.

In Great Britain, where strong camps exist both pro- and anti-South Africa, there has also been a sense of disassociation with the Republic. The embargo on arms – with notable exceptions such as the provision of Buccaneer planes with the supply of their spare parts guaranteed until 1970 – and British hostility to both white Rhodesians and white South Africans, stand in contrast to an increasing racialism in Great Britain and the emergence of racialism as a political force in the U.K. Whereas the British government sees consistency in its policy of non-

K

discrimination at home and abroad, to many English-speaking South Africans the situation smacks of hypocrisy and produces bitter remarks in Natal which would have been unthinkable a decade ago.

As a result, the 'English' section in South Africa does not look to Great Britain with the same warmth it did in Commonwealth days, and is no longer the same ideological transfer agent it once was in transmitting British thinking into the mainstream of white South African politics. While the new English supporters of the National Party do take into Afrikaner nationalism many values and concepts of their past, there is little transfer of contemporary British values. This was indicated forcibly at the time of U.D.I. when Sir de Villiers Graaff, as leader of the United Party, expressed his sympathy not for what had been 'home' to many of his supporters a decade ago, but for Ian Smith's Rhodesian Front.

When we turn to African nationalism, the story is completely different and one of closer ideological ties with the world beyond the continent. These ties are obviously not all woven into a single strand. Indeed, it is the very multiplicity of the associations which reduces many African nationalists to thinking at cross purposes. London is still the physical and emotional home of the African nationalist in exile. Like many Afrikaner nationalists, who have also read so much and so long about Britain in the largest-circulation South African newspapers, and whose lives are so patterned on English ways, Africans in the Republic have a special feeling for London that they do not have for anywhere else.

Africans from the Republic appear to find more immediate *rapport* in Britain than many who come from Asia or elsewhere in Africa. Perhaps it is because Johannesburg is a modern metropolis with a brisker pace than London; perhaps the cold, if relatively snowless, South African winter means that at least an African from Bloemfontein is not shivering for the first time as would be a man from Jamaica. The free air of permissiveness and the relative lack of a colour-bar when compared with almost any other English-speaking city in the world except Honolulu, are attractions felt by many besides Republican Africans. Were there no major barriers to the ebb and flow of Africans between Johannesburg and London, the impact of British concepts of parliamentary democracy would continue to stand foremost in African circles in South Africa. But the virtually one-way membrane through which politically active Africans pass on their way north, greatly reduces the backflow, as it was designed to do.

Nothing could be more erroneous than to consider Britain solely as a source of 'Western' influences upon African nationalism. It is pre-eminently the centre of the South African Communist Party. Its monthly journal, *The African Communist*, is in its seventh year and is not smuggled in large numbers into South Africa from London, but it serves as a forum for ideological debate within the movement. Although oriented to South Africa, it was challenged on its approach to African problems generally by the Chinese Communist slick monthly *Revolution*, published in Europe in large and expensive editions up to 1965. But as long as South African Communists remain firm supporters of the Moscow, as opposed to the Peking position, London will remain the key city.

The Soviets have not had uniform success with permanent African residents in Moscow. The language barrier is formidable and especially difficult for students. The pedagogically sound idea of Lumumba University, headed by an able Soviet educationalist, was to allow foreign students to work at their own pace in Russian and also be able to attend classes in English. Unfortunately for the Russians, what was wise educational practice looked so much like racial segregation that to many critics the institution was criticized as *Apartheid* University. Up until now neither Moscow nor Peking has nurtured revolutionaries for South Africa.

The author's conclusion in 1958[1] on the interaction between Moscow and South African Communism remains valid – namely, that the South African Communist Party is left very much to its own devices to keep itself operating. The writings of Comrade Lenin and the theoretical articles in the party press are available. Up until recently there was a steady flow of white South African Communists in and out of Moscow to personalize and refine the association, and there is still regular contact between the Communist exile group in London and Moscow.

We have discussed how the impact of Communism upon African nationalism is lessened by its transmission through white South

[1] *African Field Reports*, Cape Town, Struik, 1961, pp. 645–86.

African Communists and the continuing dominance of whites as witnessed by the large-scale planning carried on from Arthur Goldreich's Rivonia homestead before the mass capture of wanted men there by the South African police.

Concomitant with the basing of much of the African movement outside South Africa and the African continent, the splits within it have widened. The Pan African Congress is the most hydra-headed organization with a lack of co-ordination between Dar es Salaam, London, and South Africa. Ideological splits in it include Peking, Moscow, African neutralism, and London, not to mention the more – as against the lesser – militants.

Both the P.A.C. and A.N.C. have great difficulty in co-ordinating their respective sections. The problems of communication with and influence inside South Africa itself multiply the difficulties for both of them. To difficulties with the South African police are added the trouble they give each other.

The opposition party in the Transkei offers the only broad-based African opposition to the South African government based upon party organization and regular meetings. When the expansion of the role of overseas leadership is added to the suppression of the A.N.C. and the P.A.C. within South Africa, an environment is created which makes Transkei Prime Minister Kaiser Matanzima a politically exciting person to some African residents of Soweto. Sophisticated African leaders may denounce him as a 'stooge' ruling only with the bayonets of the South African government, but to many young Africans growing up in Soweto, Matanzima is the only African political figure they have heard talk or seen travel through their own community in a political parade. This generates a certain excitement and fame, irrespective of political content. It fills one kind of political vacuum. Although one cannot hold a poll to prove it as a fact, there is little doubt that Matanzima has gained markedly in active and passive African support. The figure may have only risen from 1 per cent to 20 per cent among his fellow Xhosa or, as the government would claim, to a majority, but the increase in either case is spectacular. Perhaps it is equally spectacular in the face of these difficulties if the A.N.C. and P.A.C. are rightfully able to claim adherence of most Africans. But the fact remains that the African nationalist movement is divided abroad by Western versus Communist forces; that the Communist force is divided; and that the 'tribal nationalism' of Matanzima with his policy of gaining politically against the South African government by co-operation with it in certain objectives, has gained considerable ground.

In conclusion, it is possible that the tribal nationalism and divided 'exile nationalism' will coalesce into a unified African front. It is conceivable that African and Afrikaner nationalisms might, with bloodshed and chaos, be merged into a single South African nationalism. This solution is not likely in the near future. Neither Afrikaner nor African nationalism will submit to the other. And yet few foreign observers fully assess the one and a half centuries of intimate interaction and association of Afrikaner and African in South Africa. There is a bond that will persist even under radically changed social *mores* and political patterns. The mimetic period for Afrikaners is over, and for Africans it has never fully materialized. The nationalism emerging from the southern tip of Africa will be the product of the *vleie, vlaktes,* and *kwiinduli nemilambo*[1] dear to the people of South Africa.

This view is not now acceptable to Afrikaner or African nationalists. But neither was there initial acceptance of the present equilibrium in India and Pakistan, Israel and the Arab states, or Eire and Ulster, when conflicting nationalisms had, and may still have, tragically bloody moments in longer periods of coexistence. As one who witnessed the savagery of the Belgian ejection from the Congo and the subsequent ebbing back of that element which had fled in understandable panic, the author doubts the *Götterdammerung* view often held abroad about South Africa.

Many observers anticipated '*le déluge*' would follow an unfavourable decision by the International Court of Justice on South West Africa. It was reasonable to anticipate a finding in favour of the plaintiffs, Ethiopia and Liberia, as indeed would have occurred in all likelihood if the distinguished Pakistani judge had not removed himself from the case or if the Egyptian judge had not died in the course of the trial. But it is not at all clear that a decision hostile to South Africa would have been implemented. The end of at least one phase of legal manoeuvring leaves the nationalisms in South Africa dominant in the

[1] A precise translation is not possible: approximately 'marshes', 'plains' (in Afrikaans), 'hills and rivers' (in Xhosa).

arena and more likely to influence each other than to be moulded from abroad.

The parallel evolution of Afrikaner and African nationalisms in South Africa, even when it points to African nationalism struggling with its forerunner, provides generically common experience in a predominantly Western and Christian society. Indeed, African nationalism in South Africa is more 'Western' in its organization and form, although not necessarily always in its political orientation, than African nationalisms elsewhere on the continent. The binary nature of nationalism in South Africa will persist even as it evolves into something new and South African.

INDEX

Adams College, 105

Advertisements, in African magazines, 48–49; television and, 49

Africa, effect on whites of developments in, 71, 73–74

African locations, 57

African National Congress (A.N.C.): formed (1912), 6, 28; backs Johannesburg strike (1918), 7; banned, 7; its rivalry with P.A.C., 7, 109; P.A.C. formed from, 7, 92, 100; Luthuli and, 7, 102–5; and Communism, 31, 91, 92, 93, 96, 100, 103–5, 107–8, 109, 111, 121; an underground movement, 73; does not attend All-African Convention, 86–87; supports bus boycott (1947), 99; more intellectual than P.A.C., 108

African nationalism, 1; compared with Afrikaner nationalism, 2, 7–8, 64, 81, 107–8, 117, 131; support in U.S. and U.K. for, 6; anthem of, 9–10; Indians and, 22; discards colour as a test for civilization, 24; class in, 25, 28–30; lower classes and, 29, 30; Communism and, 31, 90–92, 96, 100, 103–5, 107–8, 109–11, 129; and foreign governments, 40, 123–4, 128–9; deeper than those in the rest of Africa, 40; whites and, 41; and mass communications, 45, 55–56; its publications suppressed, 55; party organization of, 59, 60; changes in, 71, 73; stages in, 83–114; and foreign models, 85–86, 89–97, 100, 107; and Coloureds, 87–88; leaders of, 88, 107; its leaders in exile, 89, 98, 107, 109–10, 118, 123, 128, 131; lags behind other African countries, 89; its leaders feel superior to those in rest of Africa, 95–96, 107; its influence abroad, 125

African Resistance Movement (A.R.M.), 73

Africans: their first advance into South Africa halted, 1; population of, 1; their nostalgia when abroad, 12; opposed to Nazis, 14; economic goals of, 15; Pro-

gressive Party and, 20; and Afrikaners, 25, 47, 69–70; advancement of, 26; detribalized, 28, 48; in South Africa more skilful than Africans elsewhere, 29; and specialization, 29, 32, 37; immigrants from rest of Africa, 29; excluded from politics, 29–30, 82; replaced by Afrikaners on railways, 32; study Afrikaner nationalism, 33; in Civil Service, 34; in industry, 34–35, 37–38; replace whites, 35; incomes of, 35; replace Coloureds in jobs, 41; and Coloureds, 41, 42; and Indians, 41–42; their attitude to Verwoerd, 67; whites and, 73; and franchise, 86, 93–94; prosperity of, 89, 106; tribal, 112

African socialism, 89

African (tribal) reserves, 50, 51, 68, 87, 88, 97, 106

Afrikaans language, rise of, 5, 8, 58; broadcasting in, 49; 'English' and, 72, 77; university teaching in, 76; Portuguese and, 120

Afrikaner nationalism, 1; compared with African nationalism, 2, 7–8, 64, 81, 107–8, 117, 131; begins in anti-colonialism, 4, 64; rise of, 5–6; similar to European, 8; attitude of 'English' to, 19; anglicized Afrikaners and, 22; and Indians, 22; upper class in, 25; matures, 26–27, 40, 60, 70, 71; and mass communications, 45, 55; changes in, 57, 60–61, 71–72, 101; stages in, 58–82; right outflanks left in, 59, 79; foreign models for, 63–64; ex-High Commission territories and, 116–17; and Rhodesia, 122; African states and, 124; and influence abroad, 125

Afrikaners: arrive in South Africa, 1; population of, 1; and unity with 'English', 4, 13–14, 38, 42, 72, 81–82; their dislike of Britain, 9, 16, 58–59, 82; 'commandos' among, 10; and Second World War, 13, 16, 45; former inferior position of, 16, 28, 33, 38–39; changes among,